So Good To Love A Woman

So Good To Love A Woman

ISBN: 978-1-0879-8485-8

Copyright © 2021, 2024 Ohene Aku Kwapong - A PUBLICATION OF SONGHAI PUBLISHING

To the memory of my dear mother.
You gave me love.

Preface

"Loving a person could be a lot of work as you get to know them. When you find a woman that loves you, it's easy to do the work of loving her right back." -Unknown

The station was busy, alive with the steady rhythm of footsteps and the hum of voices blending into a melody of movement. I sat on the worn wooden bench, watching as people passed by—women, in all shapes and sizes, each one carrying a story, a mystery, a quiet beauty that demanded admiration. Their presence was effortless, some gliding with a grace that seemed almost otherworldly, others walking with purpose, their steps confident, deliberate. And then there were those who moved as if they were still searching, caught between the past and the future, uncertain yet still breathtaking in their own way. I should have been impatient. The train was delayed by an hour, but instead, I found myself watching, appreciating, as time slipped away unnoticed. Seeking a way to pass the time, I wandered into a nearby department store. Perhaps I'd find a new pair of shoes, a watch, something small to mark the passing of this unexpected hour. But as I strolled through the men's section, I was reminded of how dull it always was—shades of gray, black, navy, brown.

Practical. Predictable. Safe. Nothing stood out, nothing surprised me, nothing made me pause.

It wasn't until I found myself in the checkout line that my attention was truly captured. A woman stood ahead of me, holding something up to the light, her eyes flickering between curiosity and hesitation. It was silk, delicate and soft, a burst of color so vibrant it nearly shimmered. It was lingerie—bold, unapologetic, playful. She turned, her gaze locking onto mine, and in a voice laced with quiet confidence, she asked what I thought of it. I hesitated, not out of embarrassment, but because it wasn't the kind of question a man was often asked by a stranger. And yet, there was something in her eyes— something unguarded, something real. I smiled, shrugged. "What do you love about it?"

She tilted her head, surprised by the response, then smiled—a slow, knowing smile that told me she had her answer long before she ever asked the question. I have learned, over time, that women are not to be figured out or explained away in simple words. They are to be understood in the quiet moments, in the way they move, in the way they hesitate, in the way they ask a question not for an answer, but for a feeling. I have loved, I have lost, and I have come to see that every woman who has crossed my path has shaped me in ways I never expected. And so, as I walked out of that store, my hands empty but my mind full, I thought of all the women who had graced my life. Their laughter, their strength, their softness, their fire. They had been my greatest teachers, my greatest heartaches, my greatest joys.

And if I were to look back on it all, I would say this—everything I am, everything I have come to be, I owe to the women I have known.

Contents

Page Left Blank Intentionally

1

The First Touch

There were moments in my life when I found myself wondering—what if I had been born a girl? I suppose everyone has entertained that thought at least once, questioning how different their journey might have been if fate had chosen another path. Not that I ever wished to be anyone other than who I was. I was content in my boyhood, not because there was anything particularly remarkable about it, but because life, as I have lived it, has given me the privilege of curiosity. And curiosity, I have learned, is the root of every great story.

It is that curiosity—the quiet wonder of understanding the opposite sex—that has shaped the stories I am about to share with you. It is the thread that runs through the fabric of my life, weaving moments of admiration, intrigue, and lessons that I could never have learned any other way. And when I trace the beginning of that journey, I find myself in a place both distant and deeply familiar—Dunkwah, a small village on the West Coast of Africa, where the first girl I ever truly noticed left a mark on my heart that time could never erase.

I was six years old when an excruciating pain in my abdomen led to my being admitted to the local hospital. A hernia, the doctors said. Surgery was necessary. I remember my mother's face as the last thing I saw before I drifted into unconsciousness, and the first thing I saw when I awoke. The operation was a success, but the days that followed stretched endlessly, filled with nothing but the monotony of lying in bed, watching nurses—always women—come and go with little to offer a restless boy besides a kind smile and a routine check of the charts.

Then, one day, something changed.

A girl.

She must have arrived while I slept, for when I awoke, she was there, sitting quietly on the bed next to mine.

"Hello," I said, unsure if she would even respond.

She did.

And just like that, my world tilted ever so slightly on its axis.

She was the first girl I had ever spoken to outside of my sister, and there was something about her—something soft, something warm, something that, even at six years old, I knew was special. We spent our days talking, our conversations drifting into the night until sleep pulled us under. I remember the way her laughter filled the sterile hospital room, how the simple brush of her hand against mine sent a thrill through me that I didn't yet understand.

Then, all too soon, she was gone.

The day she was discharged, I cried, the loss of her presence settling into my chest like an ache I couldn't quite name. When my mother came to visit, she asked why I was so upset. I told her about the girl, about how much I had liked her, though I lacked the words to explain why.

But I remember the moment she left—how she stood in the doorway, dressed in a bright red, flowery dress, her small hand waving goodbye. The image burned itself into my memory, and even now, I see her as clearly as I did that day.

No girl has ever looked as beautiful in red as she did.

I never saw her again, and perhaps I never will. But the memory of her remains, untouched by time. And in the quiet corners of my heart, I have always believed that one day, when love finally finds me, she will wear red.

There are memories in life that, no matter how much time passes, remain as vivid as the day they happened. Some, like the first time I met a girl, have lingered in my heart like an old song playing softly in the background of my life.

For years, I asked my mother about that little girl in the hospital. Where did she go? Where might she be now? I even suggested that she try to find her, though my mother, having never met her, could do little but shake her head and smile at my persistence. But something had awakened in me then—an insatiable curiosity about girls, about who they were, about why they seemed to hold a kind of quiet magic that both fascinated and confused me.

That curiosity led me, a few years later, into one of the most embarrassing moments of my childhood.

That summer, my cousin came to stay with us. She was older, responsible for babysitting me whenever my parents went out dancing—something they did often. My mother lived for those nights, spending entire afternoons designing her outfit, ensuring every detail was perfect. And when she returned, she would recount the evening in poetic detail—the rhythm of the music, the way my father held her as they moved across the floor, the trumpeter who nearly burst a lung playing one of her favorite highlife songs. Those were magical nights for her.

3

One such evening, after my parents had left, my cousin fell asleep on the couch while I sat nearby, restless, unsure of what to do. I turned to watch her sleep, and that was when I noticed something—her body was different from mine in ways I had never paid attention to before. The curves, the shape of her face, the softness of her lips… They were all new discoveries to me. My mind raced with questions I couldn't yet put into words.

And then, I did something that would haunt me with embarrassment for years. I reached out and gently touched her chest, wondering why she had those small mounds when I did not. She stirred, her eyes fluttering open. Instead of anger, she looked at me with a knowing smile. She took my small hand, placed it back on her breast, and said, This is where babies get milk to grow.

At the time, her answer satisfied my curiosity. It wasn't until years later that the memory would come rushing back, and I would realize what I had done, how innocent yet wildly inappropriate that moment had been. And with that realization came a deep, mortified regret.

But life has a way of moving forward, sweeping you into new places, new experiences. My father's job took us to Kumasi, a city vibrant with life, where our new neighborhood, Ashanti New Town, was teeming with kids. It was there, for the first time, that I attended a coed school. Before then, my world had been filled with boys—playing with them, learning with them, talking to them. Girls had been an enigma, existing on the periphery of my awareness.

That changed the moment I stepped into my new school.

Beatrice. Mia. Frimpoma.

Three names I still remember, three faces that occupied my thoughts for months. None of them were my girlfriends, but I spent countless nights lying awake, wondering about them. What was it about them that captivated me? What would happen if I told them how much I simply enjoyed being near them?

But my teenage longing betrayed me, as all secrets eventually do.

I confided in a boy from the neighborhood—Tata. It was a mistake. Tata, ever the schemer, wasted no time in telling Frimpoma that I had a crush on her. Not only that, but he insisted we take the next step.

"We'll go see her," he said, eyes gleaming with excitement.

Frimpoma was no ordinary girl. She was the niece of the Ashanti queen mother, living in the women's section of Manhyia Palace—a place few boys dared to venture. But with Tata as my guide, I let myself be convinced.

On a warm summer evening, I told my mother I was heading to Tata's house to play. In truth, I was sneaking off to the palace— not to see the Ashanti King, but to stand before a girl who had unknowingly set my heart racing for weeks.

The palace was unlike anything I had ever seen — women everywhere, their laughter ringing through the air, their movements fluid and graceful. It was overwhelming, beautiful, almost sacred. I stood outside the gates, my heart pounding in my chest, while Tata disappeared inside to fetch Frimpoma. The plan was simple: she would come out, and I would say the words we had rehearsed—words stolen from foreign films, words that sounded romantic in theory but, in reality, required a bravery I did not possess.

"Hi, I am Ohene Aku, and I love you."

The wait felt endless, my stomach twisted in knots. And then, suddenly, she was there.

Frimpoma.

She stepped toward me, her head wrapped in a delicate scarf, her floral dress hugging her slender frame. In that moment, she was the most breathtaking girl I had ever seen.

And then, Tata did the unthinkable.

"She has something for you," he said breathlessly. "She told me she loves you too."

Time stood still. The world spun. And before I could process what was happening...

I ran.

I ran down the street like a boy being chased by a ghost, leaving Tata calling after me in confusion. I don't know if I ran because she had a gift for me, or because she had said she loved me, or because I was simply terrified of what came next. All I knew was that my feet moved before my heart could catch up.

That was the last time I ever saw Frimpoma.

Years later, I would run again—twice more, in high school—before I finally found the courage to stand still, to meet a girl's gaze without fear. But that night in Kumasi, under the moonlit sky, remains etched in my memory.

She had looked so beautiful walking toward me.

And I had run.

And to this day, I still wonder what would have happened if I had stayed.

Something had shifted in me after that night—subtle at first, but undeniable. I wouldn't have been able to name it then, but looking back, I know now that it was the beginning of something. A quiet unraveling of fear, a slow and steady curiosity taking root.

I began to feel more at ease around girls, less like a boy stumbling blindly in the dark, and more like someone trying to understand the unknown. What followed wasn't love, not yet—it was something simpler, yet no less powerful. A quest, of sorts. A need to touch, to explore, to see if the rush of a hand brushing against soft skin would make my heart race the way I imagined it would. It wasn't about desire, not in the way that older men spoke about it in hushed tones. It was about discovery. About shedding the fear that had sent me running that night.

And fate, ever a playful conspirator, placed opportunity right next door.

Beside my house was a small shop, owned by a woman who sold clothes. She had a daughter, Akosua—a girl a little older than me, with a quiet confidence that both intrigued and unsettled me. I spent more and more time at the house beside hers, where a group of girls gathered almost every evening. We'd play well into the night, laughter ringing out beneath a sky painted with moonlight. The boundaries between us were there, but they were shifting, softening.

Then came the night that changed everything.

The air was warm, the sky impossibly clear, the moon casting shadows that stretched long across the ground. It was the kind of night where the world felt alive, humming with possibility. My friend Tata showed up at my house, eyes alight with the kind of mischief that only boys on the brink of discovery could understand. Together, we went to fetch Ekow, another one of our band of restless dreamers. And then, we set off.

To the house where the girls were.

Looking back, I realize we had planned this. Not in any sinister way, but with the kind of quiet intention that boys our age carried in their hearts. We weren't chasing love. We weren't even chasing passion. We were chasing a feeling—the rush of skin against skin, the whispered thrill of a stolen moment.

We wanted to know what it felt like to touch a girl.

Not for any reason other than the simple, undeniable truth that we had never done it before. And that night, beneath a sky full of stars, we were determined to find out.

The evening air was thick with the scent of woodsmoke and the lingering warmth of a sun that had long since dipped below the horizon. It was a night like any other, full of the nervous excitement that came with being young, reckless, and foolish enough to believe we had love all figured out.

Our plan was simple, if not entirely honorable. We'd linger near the girls as they went about their evening chores, waiting for the moment one of us could pull one of them aside. The trick was to convince her that someone—a brave fool standing in the shadows of the backyard—had a message just for her. And then, it was up to him to make his move.

8

When my turn came, I barely hesitated. Heart pounding, I dashed through the dark, breathless with anticipation rather than fear. I was ready. Or so I thought.

I remember glancing down, double-checking the safety pin that held my braces to my shorts. Everything was in place, at least physically. But as I stood there, panting, excitement mingling with uncertainty, something unexpected happened.

A sudden, unmistakable tightness in my pants.

And then, there was Akosia, walking toward me with an ease that only made my panic worse. I had seconds to react, and instinct took over—I clutched my hands over my crotch, a futile attempt at concealing what I barely understood myself.

She stopped in front of me, waiting. Expecting.

I had seen this scene unfold before—not in real life, but on a flickering screen during stolen movie nights at boarding school. I should have known what to do. But the truth was, no one had ever told me exactly how to be with a girl in the dark.

So I did the only thing I could think of. I wrapped my arms around her, pressed myself against her thighs, and giggled like a boy who had found himself in a dream he wasn't quite ready for.

She pulled back, eyes curious. "What are you doing?"

I froze.

The certainty I had felt mere minutes ago unraveled. Whatever script I had been following was clearly the wrong one. Shame crawled up my spine, and I stepped back, dropping my hands to my sides.

But then—she reached for me.

With a quiet confidence that both terrified and intrigued me, she guided my hands to the curve of her hips, then to the roundness of her backside. Her fingers slid up, wrapping around my neck, and before I could even process what was happening, her lips pressed against mine.

I should have been elated. Thrilled. But instead, a storm of questions raged in my mind. How did she know how to do this? Had she done it before? Was she—

Panic flared, hot and sudden. Without thinking, I pulled away and bolted.

The night air burned in my lungs as I ran, my friends' laughter echoing behind me before I even reached them. They demanded to know why I had fled, why I had thrown away the very opportunity they would have killed for.

"She's a bad girl," I stammered, still breathless. "She knew how to do… things."

Their laughter deepened, rich with the knowledge I had yet to grasp. I had been given the moment every boy dreamed of, and I had thrown it away.

Even now, I can't recall ever seeing that girl again. She never became a friend, never even became a memory beyond that one night. And maybe that's how I know—I had never wanted her. Not really. I had only wanted the idea of her. The experience.

But love, I would later learn, is never just an idea. It is real, raw, and terrifying in ways no boy is ever prepared for.

The years passed in quiet transition, moving me from one school to the next, from coed to all-boys, as my family settled into yet another place, another chapter. This time, it was a boarding school by the Atlantic, closer to the capital, where the waves crashed endlessly against the shore, a constant reminder that time never stood still.

I had never been in love. Not truly. Not in the way the novels described, where hearts raced and souls intertwined in something deep and inescapable. But in an all-boys school, the only way to understand girls, to imagine what love might feel like, was through books. And so, I read—devoured romance novels that painted a world I had yet to experience. In those pages, I learned about longing, about the weight of a single glance, about the ache of a touch not yet given.

It was an exciting time, though all theoretical, until I met Mia.

She was unexpected. A moment that crept into my life without warning, like the first warm breeze of harmattan, carrying the scent of something new, something unexplored.

We had moved again, to a neighborhood where, as fate would have it, the house next door was home to a group of teenage girls, all around my age. And among them was Mia—elegant, sharp-witted, and entirely unlike anyone I had ever met.

She fascinated me, not just for her beauty, which was undeniable, but for her mind. She was quick, sarcastic, and unafraid to challenge me. Until then, intelligence had always been something I associated with the boys I knew—the ones who debated philosophy late into the night or calculated mathematical problems with ease. But Mia was different. She was proof that brilliance was not confined to a single gender. She saw the world with depth, with curiosity, and with a confidence that made me question everything I thought I knew about attraction.

She had a boyfriend—of course, she did. A rich man's son, the kind who had the effortless charm of someone who never had to chase what he wanted. He drove his father's Mercedes-Benz, while I walked or took the bus, a difference that felt insurmountable at the time.

And yet, we became friends. We spent time together, visiting each other's homes, talking for hours.

Then, one day, she invited me over.

I was fifteen. The invitation itself felt like something out of the novels I had read, full of unspoken meaning. When I arrived, she took me up to her room, where I lay on her bed, listening as she talked about her boyfriend—how she didn't really find him attractive, how, surprisingly, she was into me.

For the life of me, I didn't know what to do with that.

I should have been thrilled. Any other boy would have seen the moment for what it was—an open door, an opportunity. But I was young, uncertain, still learning the language of love, and I had no script for what came next.

New Year's Eve of 1978. The night she came to visit me at my house.

She had written me a letter, one she planned to give me that night. I hadn't known that then. I had only known that she was there, with me, and that something lingered between us— something unspoken, something weighty.

In my nervousness, I tried to kiss her. It was clumsy, awkward, a fumbled attempt at translating feeling into action. Whatever magic had been there before, whatever intention she had carried with her that night, disappeared in an instant.

She left soon after, but she left the letter behind.

It wasn't until I unfolded the pages, my heart pounding as I read, that I understood what the night had truly been about.

She had fallen in love with me. And she had come that night to give herself to me, to surrender her innocence in a way that, at the time, I hadn't been able to grasp.

But something had shifted in her, in us. The awkwardness of that kiss, my inability to meet the moment with the same certainty she had, made her rethink everything.

And just like that, what could have been vanished, lost to time, to inexperience, to the weight of a moment neither of us was truly ready for.

In the end, it all worked out the way it was meant to. My friendship with Mia—one that I still treasure to this day—might not have been what it is had things gone differently that night. Once the awkwardness faded, we found our rhythm again, and our time together became something truly special. Her company sharpened my mind, put my fears about girls to rest, and gave me something I hadn't expected—an intellectual companionship that was both rare and deeply fulfilling.

We spent hours in libraries, lost in discussions about books, philosophy, life itself. What we had was pure, untainted by the pressure to turn it into something romantic. And in that way, it was more valuable than I could have ever imagined at the time.

But romance wasn't done with me yet. And neither was heartbreak.

It wasn't long after that I met Joyce. She lived just across from Mia, though they weren't particularly friends. She was introduced to me by Moon Tiger, a neighborhood friend who would soon become my partner in mischief, the kind of friend who made life more thrilling and dangerous in equal measure.

One afternoon, Moon Tiger and I found ourselves at Joyce's house. She had invited us over, knowing her father was at work and that we would have the place to ourselves. For forty-five blissful minutes, we sat there, talking, laughing, feeling the kind of invincibility that only comes with youth.

And then, we heard it.

The sudden grind of gates being pushed open, the unmistakable sound of tires rolling onto the driveway.

Her father was home.

Had someone seen us? Had he sensed something? We didn't have time to wonder. Joyce, wide-eyed and panicked, pushed us up the stairs, leading us through a hidden passageway that opened onto the roof.

The sun was merciless. The corrugated iron burned beneath our hands, lizards scuttled around us, and the heat pressed down on us like a punishment. We stayed there for three hours, silent and sweating, listening as her father had his lunch, took his siesta, and eventually, as if satisfied that nothing was amiss, got back into his car and left.

When we finally climbed down, we thought for sure she'd want us gone. But she didn't.

14

Instead, she wanted to stay with me, as if nothing had happened. As if, in that moment, her choice had been made.

She liked me. Just like Mia had. But unlike Mia, she had no boyfriend, no rich man's son pulling her in another direction.

I never imagined I would have choices. That girls—two girls—would look at me that way. But that realization, that feeling of possibility, made me hunger for more. I was finally ready to explore what I had only daydreamed about for so long.

And so, the next weekend, Moon Tiger introduced me to another girl—Jennifer.

Jennifer was the daughter of a police officer, which should have been my first warning. Visiting her at home was a risk, and I hesitated, telling Moon Tiger I wasn't sure about this one. But he convinced me, and I went.

And I am so glad I did.

Jennifer was unlike the others. There was something about her—something calm, almost ethereal. She exuded innocence in a way that made her presence feel like a comfort rather than a challenge.

And when I kissed her, something shifted inside me.

It was my first real kiss—the kind that stays with you forever, not just for the feeling of lips against lips, but for the way time seemed to slow, the way the air thickened around us, as if the world itself was holding its breath. There was something else, too. A taste—something sweet, something unexplainable, a memory imprinted so deeply that even now, I can summon it like a whisper from the past.

When we finally pulled away, she smiled and told me she had to travel to see her mother. She promised to visit me when she got back.

But she never did.

The news came like a blow I wasn't prepared for.

A bus accident. Gone. Just like that.

I had only known her for a few hours, but it was enough. Enough to feel the loss settle deep, to wonder what could have been, to wish—fiercely, desperately—that I could get that moment back.

But life doesn't work that way.

At the time, I didn't fully understand what had happened. I don't think I processed it the way I should have. How could I? I was still a boy, still learning how to navigate the world, still trying to grasp what it meant to lose something before it had the chance to become anything at all.

And so, I did what young boys do. I moved forward. I carried on. But the past never truly leaves us.

Boarding school, with its walls lined with restless boys, only made the absence of girls more profound. And absence, as they say, makes the heart grow fonder.

In those long months surrounded by nothing but male voices, my thoughts kept drifting back—to Mia, to Joyce, to Jennifer. To the intrigue, the thrill, the mystery of it all.

I had touched something real, something fleeting. And even in its brevity, it had changed me.

I would never look at love the same way again.

I wondered—we all did—if girls talked about boys the way we talked about them.

Did they sit in circles, whispering about what it felt like to have a boy's hand brush against theirs? Did they giggle over the thrill of a first kiss, dissecting every moment the way we did? Did they wonder, as we did, what it meant to be wanted?

As I later learned, they did.

Girls talked about boys just as much as boys talked about girls. They were just as curious, just as eager to understand the mystery of the opposite sex. The difference, though, lay in the way we spoke about it.

Boys, in their bravado, masked their emotions with jokes, turning feelings into something to be mocked rather than explored. Love, affection—these were things to be laughed at, to be reduced to teasing and playful jabs. There was a lack of sensitivity in how we handled something so fragile, something I was beginning to realize had depth beyond the surface.

Because for me, touching a girl, kissing a girl—those moments had meant something.

They weren't just stories to tell; they were experiences that had begun to shape me, teaching me that attraction was more than just a rush of adrenaline. It was a connection, a moment of vulnerability, a shared secret between two people that lingered long after the touch had faded.

And yet, for years after, that was my story.

The memory of the girl I had kissed, of the moments I had stolen before high school, became the tale I told when the boys wanted to know where I had come from, what kind of world I had known before boarding school.

It was proof that I had lived, that I had touched something real, even if I didn't yet fully understand what it all meant.

2

Would You Come to the Dance?

Some moments in life stay with you forever. For me, it was the nights my parents spent dancing under the open sky, their laughter carried away by the breeze, their bodies swaying effortlessly to the rhythm of the live band. I was just a boy then, watching from the sidelines, captivated by the magic of it all. The way my father held my mother close, the way she smiled up at him—it was the kind of love that felt untouchable, something out of a storybook.

But love, I would come to learn, isn't just about grand moments. Sometimes, it's about the quiet longing, the waiting, the search for something as simple as a dance.

My search lasted longer than I ever expected. Through middle school and high school, I watched from afar, unsure, hesitant. I had grown up with the image of my mother twirling beneath the stars, and I longed for my own moment—to hold someone close, to move in sync with another heartbeat. But reality had a way of making things complicated.

Before I could take that first step onto the dance floor, life took me on a different kind of journey. My family moved to Kumasi, and I found myself struggling to belong in a coed middle school, the faces around me unfamiliar, the distractions endless. My parents saw my restlessness, my inability to focus, and in an attempt to set things right, they sent me to Salem Boys Boarding School.

Salem was structured, disciplined, a place where I could steady myself. But even there, curiosity found me. Every Sunday, we attended service at the Presbyterian Church, where our voices rose in song, our prayers filled the air. For the longest time, it was only us—the boys. That was until the day the girls from Demonstration School arrived.

They sat separately, as was expected. But their presence changed everything. Heads turned mid-prayer, whispers spread through the pews like ripples in water. And for the first time in my life, I understood that some dances don't begin with music. Sometimes, they begin with a glance across a church aisle, a heartbeat quickening in anticipation.

And sometimes, they begin long before you even realize you've been waiting for them all along.

As the days in boarding school stretched into weeks, then months, our habits evolved, shifting like the seasons. Some routines lasted only a few days, others became rituals that lingered for weeks. And then there were the obsessions—the small, unexpected comforts that kept us tethered to something beyond the high walls of Salem.

For me, it was love songs.

In a world where real conversations with girls were nothing more than a distant dream, music became my bridge to an experience I had yet to live. The lyrics, the melodies, the aching sincerity in every word—love songs were my window into something beautiful, something untouchable. I clung to them, memorized them, wrote the verses down on pages as if by knowing the words, I could understand the feelings they described.

Roberta Flack's Killing Me Softly became my anthem. I must have played it in my mind a thousand times, each line carving its way into me like poetry I wasn't meant to forget. And I wasn't alone in this obsession. On Friday nights, a few of us from the dorms would gather, our notebooks filled with lyrics, our voices rising together in quiet harmony. We weren't just singing; we were dreaming—of love, of connection, of something beyond the rigid structure of our days.

But for all its camaraderie, boarding school was missing something. The absence of girls was one thing, but it was the absence of home that truly weighed on me. I missed my mother's gentle voice, my sister's laughter echoing through the house. I missed the warmth of familiarity, the ease of being surrounded by love that asked for nothing in return.

And so, one day, I ran.

It wasn't planned, wasn't something I had ever imagined myself doing. I wasn't the boy who broke rules or rebelled against authority. But homesickness doesn't follow logic, and neither does longing. Before I knew it, I was gone, my feet carrying me away from the dormitories, from the disciplined order of school life, straight toward the only place that had ever felt like home.

Looking back, I suppose it was inevitable. You can only hold onto a song for so long before you need something real. And in that moment, home was the only thing that felt real to me.

There was always something about girls that fascinated me. It wasn't just attraction, though that was there in its own quiet way. It was more than that—a feeling, a presence, an energy that seemed to shift the air around them. Being near them, hearing their laughter, watching the way they moved through the world—it was like stepping into a different kind of magic, one I didn't fully understand but desperately wanted to.

Yes, as I grew older, desire lived somewhere in the background, a part of me I was just beginning to acknowledge. But it wasn't what drove me. What I wanted—what I had always wanted—was simple: a dance. Just one dance, where I could hold someone close, where the music would wrap around us like a secret only we could hear. It wasn't about anything more than that. It was curiosity, wonder, and the unshakable belief that there was something extraordinary in the simple act of moving with another person.

When the time came to choose a secondary school, I knew my decision wasn't just about academics or reputation. It was about opportunity. My two older brothers had attended a boys' boarding school, and my sister had gone to a coed secondary school. That fact alone puzzled me. My parents had always been strict, especially when it came to my sister. And yet, they had allowed her to be in an environment where boys and girls coexisted, something they had never been willing to allow at home.

My father, in particular, was firm in his rules. Girls visiting our house was out of the question. I still remember the day he walked into a room and found my ten-year-old brother sitting alone with a girl his age. The anger on his face was unforgettable, his voice sharp as he told my mother he wouldn't allow his sons to have girls over. It was a rule as unbreakable as any in our home.

And yet, despite growing up in that atmosphere, I was determined. I had spent too long watching from the sidelines, waiting for the right moment. High school was my chance, my moment to step into a world where maybe, just maybe, I could finally gather the courage to ask someone to dance.

I graduated from middle school on time, leaving behind the mundane, predictable days that had shaped me in quiet, unremarkable ways. The future was now open, filled with the thrill of possibility. Two high schools had accepted me—one was coed, the other an all-boys boarding school. For the longest time, I had planned to go to the coed school. It felt like the natural choice, a chance to be in a world where I wouldn't have to wait for a weekend dance to be around girls.

But then I found out that my next-door neighbor—a girl I had never particularly liked because she was loud and always seemed to fill the air with her presence—had decided to attend the same school. And just like that, I changed my mind.

I chose the all-boys school instead.

In hindsight, it was a foolish attempt to outrun something I didn't even fully understand. Because if I thought a boys' school would temper my newfound fascination with girls, I was sorely mistaken. High school brought new experiences, new faces, and most excitingly—new possibilities. Even though we were separated from girls during the day, they were never far from our minds.

Every weekend, our school held dances, inviting girls from different schools to join us. The moment Friday arrived, a single thought consumed me: Will I finally get my first dance?

And so the years that followed became a rhythm of anticipation, each one lived from one weekend to the next, always waiting, always wondering—Would this be the night? Would I find a girl who would hold my hand, who would dance with me under the dim lights of the school hall, who might even, if I was lucky, love me in return?

To my relief, I wasn't the only one plagued by such thoughts. By my second year, I had formed a bond with a group of boys who shared the same longing. We became a brotherhood of sorts, a quiet, unspoken love cabal, where we spent nights listening to love songs, carefully writing down the lyrics as if by understanding the words, we could understand love itself.

Saturday nights were our salvation. Entertainment nights, dances, club outings to girls' schools—these were the moments we lived for. They were free and easy, filled with possibility, until I joined the school pop band in my second year.

That was when everything changed.

Being in the band meant being on stage. It meant girls noticing me in ways they never had before. It meant, for the first time, I was no longer just an observer—I was part of the spectacle.

And with that realization came the second stage of my education in girls. Up until then, I had admired them from a distance, longing without knowing how to act on it. But now, I was suddenly in their world, a world I had spent so much time running from, only to find that perhaps, I had been running toward it all along.

The invitation came as a surprise. Our school pop band had been asked to play at the University of Science and Technology in Kumasi, part of a grand university dance program. It was an opportunity—one I should have been excited about. And yet, the moment I heard the news, all I felt was fear.

This would be my first time performing in front of such a large audience—over a hundred people, students far older than I was, sophisticated and confident in ways I could only imagine. The thought of standing on that stage, under the glare of lights, sent a nervous tremor through me. But the seniors in the band reassured me, their easy confidence like a lifeline. We'll be with you the whole time, they said. And somehow, I believed them.

We arrived at the venue early, hours ahead of the performance, to set up. The band leader, Solo, introduced us to his older sister, a university student. She was friendly, composed in that effortless way older girls seemed to be, and when I mentioned needing a glass of water, she smiled and offered to get me something to eat.

"Come with me," she said.

And so I did. Without thinking, without asking where we were going, without understanding that sometimes, when a girl asks you to follow her, you should always—always—ask, Where are we going?

I followed her across campus, past students walking in small clusters, past the hum of conversations I didn't belong to. And then we arrived at Africa Hall.

I stopped cold.

It was a sea of girls.

I had never—never—seen so many girls in one place in my entire life. It felt like I had stumbled into some secret world, a place I was never meant to enter. My mind flashed back to childhood, to the day I had wandered into the women's section of the Manhyia Palace, overwhelmed by the sheer presence of royal women dressed in intricate cloth, their voices soft but commanding. That same stunned feeling overtook me now.

I couldn't move forward.

"I'm not coming in," I blurted out.

Solo's sister turned, confused. I could see the question forming on her lips, but I couldn't answer it. What would I say? That I was terrified? That the sight of so many beautiful girls had made my pulse quicken and my stomach twist into knots? Instead, I muttered something about a stomachache and feeling like I might vomit.

That was what saved me—though saved me from what, I wasn't entirely sure.

I had no clear idea what made a girl beautiful. I had never been close enough to one long enough to know. But in that moment, at the entrance of Africa Hall, I realized something—I could feel beauty. It was in the way they moved, the way they carried themselves, each one different from the next. Some walked with deliberate grace, others with a carefree rhythm. Their hands swung at their sides, their laughter wove through the air like a melody I didn't know the words to.

And yet, for all my fascination, something held me back. The memory of the Manhyia Palace lingered in my mind, a beautiful yet burdensome weight. It had sparked in me a curiosity about girls, a longing to understand them. But here, now, in the presence of so many, that same curiosity felt paralyzing.

I turned away, retreating into the safety of what was familiar, my heartbeat still racing, my breath still unsteady.

Africa Hall would remain a mystery.

For now.

After a few minutes, the initial shock of it all began to fade, and in its place, a slow, knowing smile crept across my face. What I had just witnessed—what I had just survived—was nothing short of extraordinary. I had seen something that none of the boys back in the dorms had ever laid eyes on, a discovery so grand it demanded to be told with the kind of awe and exaggeration that would keep them hanging onto every word.

Africa Hall.

A place filled with more beautiful girls than I had ever imagined possible.

Oh, they were going to eat this up.

Just as I was piecing together the grand tale I would tell, Solo's sister reappeared, carrying a piece of buttered bread and a glass of water. She handed them to me with a kind smile, then sat beside me as I ate, her presence steady, unfazed by my earlier reluctance. She seemed to know every girl who passed by, greeting them with an ease I envied. And as she exchanged pleasantries with them, my every bite of bread seemed to land in rhythm with her words, as if I was digesting not just food, but the very moment itself.

I ate slowly, deliberately, stretching the experience for as long as I could.

When I finished, she stood, ready to walk me back to the concert hall.

As we moved through campus, my mind was already working overtime, crafting the narrative I would deliver to the boys. It had to be unbelievable yet convincing, grand yet sprinkled with just enough truth to keep them hooked. I could see it now—the circle of eager faces in the dorm, eyes wide with envy, hanging onto my every word as I described the sheer number of girls, the way they walked, the way they looked, the way I had somehow stumbled into this moment of pure, once-in-a-lifetime fortune.

I was lucky.

Blessed, even.

We arrived at the concert hall just as my school's pop band was getting ready to take the stage. The timing was perfect. But before I could slip back into my role as just another band member, Solo turned to me, his brow furrowed in curiosity.

"Why did you take so long?"

And there it was—the moment of truth. The chance to spin a story so fantastic it would become legend.

I opened my mouth, ready to tell him something, anything. But then, just as quickly, I hesitated.

Because the truth was, I lacked the courage to lie.

And so, I simply shrugged, offering nothing but a vague smile, as if what had happened was too great, too sacred, to put into words.

Let them wonder.

Let them dream about what I had seen.

For some things, I realized, were better left a mystery.

I was fifteen years old, a bassist in the school pop band, probably the youngest kid to ever play the bass—just about five feet tall, which meant I was barely taller than my own instrument when it stood upright. But that night, none of it mattered. We played to thunderous applause, the kind that shakes the walls, the kind that makes you forget your fears and believe, if only for a moment, that you belong up there on stage.

And when the final note faded, when we took our bows under the bright lights, I noticed something I hadn't expected—the seniors in the band pointing at me.

It took a second to register, but then I understood. The applause, the cheers, the standing ovation—it was for me.

A thrill ran through me, the kind of electric rush I imagined one might feel standing at the edge of a cliff just before leaping into the unknown. I kept bowing, over and over, drinking in the moment as if it might never come again. I wanted to stay in that applause forever. But soon enough, we were ushered off the stage, the moment slipping away like sand through my fingers.

Then, just as I was stepping down from the stage, I felt a tap on my shoulder.

I turned. It was Solo, the same kid whose sister had fed me earlier. His expression was unreadable, but his words were clear.

"Come with me. Some of the university students want to meet you."

I hesitated for only a second before following him, my heart still soaring from the performance. We walked toward the side entrance of the hall, my mind still half-lost in the glow of the stage. But then, without warning, Solo stopped, turned slightly, and gestured toward a group waiting nearby.

I followed his gaze.

It was a group of girls. University girls. Older girls. Beautiful girls.

And they were all looking at me.

It happened in an instant—one second, I was standing there, feeling like I was on top of the world, and the next, sheer panic overtook me. My feet moved before my brain could stop them. I took off running.

I don't remember much after that.

I ran so fast, so blindly, that the world blurred around me. I ran through campus, past buildings I didn't recognize, past people I would never see again. All I knew was that I had to get away.

At some point, I must have stopped, must have found someone willing to take pity on the frantic boy who had clearly lost his way. Because the next thing I knew, I was back at school, dropped off by a stranger from whom I had hitchhiked a ride.

I sat on my bed that night, staring at the ceiling, knowing—knowing—that I was ruined.

The heroic story I had planned to tell—the grand tale of discovering a bevy of beautiful girls, of confidently chatting with them for hours, of maybe, just maybe, leaving with the beginnings of something unforgettable—was now worthless.

Because my schoolmates had seen me.

They had watched me run, had likely laughed as I disappeared into the night.

For months, I kept my mouth shut, consumed by humiliation. Was it shyness? Was it actual fear? I didn't know. All I knew was that I loved talking about girls, loved watching them from a distance, loved wondering about them. And yet, when faced with them, when given the chance to actually be in their presence, something inside me failed.

But one thing was certain—I wasn't done trying.

As the days, weeks, and months passed, I waited for a chance to redeem myself.

And just before summer recess, fate, merciful as ever, gave me exactly that.

First Dance That Almost Never Was

Dance Night was a ritual, a promise of magic that arrived every Saturday at precisely 4:00 p.m. Like clockwork, the girls would appear in groups, their teachers hovering nearby as chaperones, ensuring that every laugh, every stolen glance, remained within the bounds of propriety.

The brave boys—the ones who carried themselves with easy confidence—would walk up to the girls and ask for a dance. The not-so-brave? Well, they danced with each other, moving awkwardly in the corners of the room, pretending they didn't mind.

And then there was me.

For two years, I sat and watched. Two whole years. I never asked. Never dared. The words—so simple, so small—never made it past my lips: May I have this dance?

I watched boys and girls spinning across the floor, laughter rising above the music, the unspoken language of youth and curiosity weaving between them. And yet, every Saturday, I let another chance slip away, waiting for something—anything—to push me past the fear that had held me back for so long.

And then, when I least expected it, the opportunity arrived.

It was the last semester dance at St. Louis Secondary School—
an all-girls boarding school. This was more than just a dance. It
was a school-wide debate competition between our two schools,
followed by a DJ-sponsored event where, for once, fear would
not win.

This was it.

This was going to be the night.

But there was one problem.

A group of us from the dorm wanted to go, but we couldn't
afford the transportation and the entry fee for the dance. The
weight of our disappointment settled heavily on us, but giving up
wasn't an option. If we had to scheme our way in, then so be it.

The school had set up a foolproof system—or so they thought.
Everyone who paid received a stamp on their left palm the
morning of the event, a mark that granted them passage into the
dance.

There were six of us. Only one of us, Blankson, could afford the
ticket. But instead of accepting defeat, we hatched what we
believed was a genius plan.

Blankson paid the fee, received his stamp, and then rushed back
to the dorm, where we were waiting like a group of masterminds
plotting a grand heist. We had prepared for this moment—a
bottle of gentian violet and freshly sliced pieces of cassava lay in
front of us.

We studied the ink on Blankson's palm, the intricate curves, the
slight smudges where the stamp had settled into his skin. Then,
with careful precision, we pressed the stamp onto the soft flesh
of the cassava slices, letting them absorb every detail.

One by one, we transferred the ink onto our own palms, pressing down, holding our breath.

When we were done, we inspected our work.

Perfect.

So flawless, in fact, that even we couldn't tell the difference between our makeshift stamps and the real thing.

We were going to that dance.

And for the first time in my life, I was finally going to ask a girl to dance.

When the bus arrived, we were first in line, our hands steady, our hearts pounding. This was the moment of truth. Would our makeshift stamps hold up under scrutiny? Would the plan we had crafted so carefully fall apart at the very last moment?

But then—just like that—we were waved on.

The student checking stamps barely glanced at our hands before motioning us forward. No suspicion, no second looks, no idea that he had just admitted a few eager stowaways into what, for us, felt like the grandest adventure of our teenage lives.

The bus was packed, the air buzzing with anticipation. As we pulled away from the school, I let out a breath I hadn't realized I was holding. Relief washed over me. We had done it. We were going.

And then, reality hit.

What the hell was I doing?

Had I really gone through all of this just to freeze up again? To sit in a corner, too afraid to speak, too nervous to ask for a dance? Was I really going to let another opportunity slip through my fingers?

The thought gnawed at me, circling my mind like a restless ghost.

That's when Slim, my friend from the school band, nudged me.

"What's bothering you?" he asked.

I hesitated. Slim and I were the same age, but in matters concerning girls, he was light-years ahead of me. He had a confidence about him, a way of speaking to girls that was so effortless it felt almost unfair. If there was anyone who could help me navigate this night, it was him.

So, for the first time, I let it all out.

I told him about my fears, about how I had spent years admiring girls from a distance but never once had the courage to actually talk to them, let alone dance with them. I admitted that every time I got close, I panicked, my body betraying me, my feet carrying me away before I could even try.

Slim listened, nodding thoughtfully, his expression unreadable.

The bus rumbled forward, carrying us closer to St. Louis Secondary School, closer to the dance floor, closer to my moment of reckoning.

And as we pulled up to the gates, I knew—I could count on Slim.

Because if anyone could come up with a plan to make sure I didn't run away this time, it was him.

As we stepped off the bus, the night stretched before us, full of promise and possibility. My pulse quickened, not just from excitement but from the silent battle still waging inside me— Would I finally do it? Would I finally ask a girl to dance?

Slim, ever the confident one, pulled Blankson and me aside, his expression unreadable.

"I have something for you," he said, his voice low, conspiratorial.

Blankson and I exchanged glances, intrigued.

"This will make you bold," Slim continued. "So bold that you'll be able to walk up to any girl and ask her to dance. No hesitation. No fear. It'll make you fearless of women."

Fearless.

That was all I needed to hear.

Neither of us had ever truly understood why girls intimidated us so much. It wasn't something we could name or define. It was just… there. A force that turned our legs to lead, that sent our thoughts scattering like leaves in the wind.

But if Slim had the cure, if he had found a way to rid us of whatever mysterious spell girls had over us, then who was I to question him?

Without hesitation, I took the two tiny white pills he handed me, popped them into my mouth, and swallowed.

It felt like the answer to a prayer.

With that, we strode into the debate hall, confidence flooding through us, certain that by the end of the night, we would be the boys everyone talked about—the ones who danced with the most girls, who turned heads, who left no opportunity untaken.

The debate was supposed to be a mere formality, a necessary prelude to the real event—the dance. But as I sat there, waiting, the words of the debaters stretched endlessly, blurring together, their voices lulling me into a strange, slow rhythm.

Something was wrong.

I blinked. The stage in front of me seemed to tilt. I turned my head—Slim was gone.

I looked to my right.

Blankson was slumped against a wall, his head drooping, his eyelids heavy.

And then it hit me.

My own body felt sluggish, my limbs impossibly weighted. As I tried to stand, a wave of drowsiness washed over me. The room, once so full of anticipation, now seemed softer, hazier.

My feet moved forward, but my mind drifted backward, as if wading through water.

I squinted across the room.

Had there always been that many girls?

They seemed to multiply, their movements slow and dreamlike, their laughter distant, like an echo from another world.

And then it dawned on me.

Slim had given us sleeping pills.

I barely made it to the back of the room before my body gave up the fight. I collapsed, the world spinning one last time before everything faded to black.

Somewhere, in the midst of the music and the laughter, Blankson and I slept like babies—dead to the world, dead to the dance we had fought so hard to attend.

By the time we woke up, we were already back at school.

We had no memory of how we got on the bus, no stories of stolen glances, no triumphant tales of our first dance.

Nothing.

Just humiliation.

I cringed at the thought of how my friends must have laughed at us, the great adventure that had turned into this—a wasted night, a grand failure.

And Slim?

Well, Slim turned out to be less of a mastermind and more of a prankster, the kind of kid you quickly learn not to trust.

That night was not going to be the night I conquered my fear of girls. But maybe, just maybe, the next opportunity would be different.

OHENE AKU KWAPONG

3

Could Tonight Be the Night?

There was a time in my life when the world seemed divided neatly into two: boys and girls. And in my world, boys stuck with boys. We ran in packs, laughed at jokes only we understood, and shielded ourselves from the mysteries of the opposite sex. It was safe, predictable—even comforting. But what I didn't realize then was that this shield, this invisible wall of camaraderie, was also keeping me from something essential. It was keeping me from growing into the kind of man I wanted to be—the kind who understood the art of conversation, the unspoken dance of courtship, and the quiet thrill of catching someone's eye across the room.

Blankson and I learned that lesson the hard way. Our last visit to the girls' school had ended in embarrassment, a lesson in humility we hadn't signed up for. But it also sparked an idea—one that, if executed properly, might change everything. What if we hosted our own dance? What if, for one night, we created a space where boys like us—who weren't the loudest or the most confident—stood a chance?

The trick, of course, was making it official. No girl was going to accept an invitation from two unknown boys. We needed something that carried weight. A plan began to form: an invitation, not from us, but from our headmaster himself. Or at least, that's what the letter would suggest. If we could deliver it to their headmistress, we just might pull this off.

That's how I found myself, on a warm afternoon, standing at the entrance of the girls' school, the letter in my hand, my pulse unsteady. As we waited, a girl—one of the students—stepped forward to greet us. She had an easy confidence, the kind that made conversation feel effortless. Before I knew it, we were talking. About the things that made her laugh. About the kind of boys she liked. About the ones she'd consider dancing with, and the ones she wouldn't.

I don't know how long we talked—maybe an hour, maybe three. Time seemed to slip away in the warmth of her voice, in the way she tilted her head when she listened. And then, just before I left, I did something I had never done before. I asked her to come as my guest.

There was a shift in the air, something almost imperceptible. A small moment, but one that felt impossibly significant. Maybe, just maybe, this was where it all changed. Maybe this was the moment I stopped letting fear dictate the narrative.

And yet, one question remained. Would she come? Would tonight be the night I finally stepped across that invisible line?

I supposed I would find out soon enough.

A Night That Changed Everything

After weeks of anticipation, the evening had finally arrived. We had spent so much time planning—drafting letters, scheming with the DJ, imagining how the night would unfold—that it felt almost surreal to stand there, waiting.

And then, just before eight, the girls started arriving. At first, in hesitant trickles, but soon, in groups. More than we had expected. The room filled with laughter and the kind of nervous excitement that comes when you know something unforgettable is about to happen.

Everything was going according to plan. The DJ set the tone with upbeat dance songs, a perfect way to ease into the night. But our true strategy lay in what came next: the switch to slow songs, the moment we'd been waiting for. That was when we'd get our real chance—to hold someone close, to feel, if only for a few minutes, what it was like to belong to someone.

And yet, despite all my preparation, despite the girl I had spent an entire afternoon talking to, the girl I had invited as my guest, I didn't look for her. I didn't search the crowd, didn't wait in anxious hope to see her walk through the door. Because the truth was, in that moment, surrounded by so many girls, so many better-looking girls, I forgot her entirely.

It was like stepping into a dream where anything was possible, where I had too many choices and not enough sense to know which one mattered. I moved from one girl to the next, unable to settle, caught up in the intoxicating thrill of possibility.

Eventually, I landed on someone—an attractive girl who, for all her beauty, was a stranger to me. I barely knew her, and yet, all I could think about was finding a quiet, dark corner where I could steal a kiss, where I could feel the rush of something forbidden and new.

But the moment didn't unfold the way I had imagined. There was no spark, no warmth in her touch. And when we finally found a secluded bench, just as I was about to close the space between us, a voice cut through the night.

"Get the hell out of there!"

The night watchman.

In an instant, everything shattered. The girl bolted, her silhouette vanishing into the shadows. I ran too, my pulse racing, my mind reeling.

I never saw her again.

And just like that, the night ended—not in triumph, not in romance, but in an empty kind of disappointment. The dance I had dreamed of, the connection I had hoped to find, never happened. Instead, I was left with something unexpected, something uncomfortable.

For the first time, I understood that attraction was more than just beauty. That whatever I had been searching for couldn't be found in a stolen kiss with a stranger.

The months that followed were restless and uncertain. I found myself searching, not for another dance, not for another fleeting thrill, but for something real. For someone who felt like home.

That summer, I returned home to familiar faces and familiar streets. And, of course, to Joyce.

She had always been there, the girl next door. Our families had woven a quiet expectation around us, a whispered assumption that one day, when we were older, we would marry.

For years, I had believed it too.

But that summer—the summer of my third year of high school—everything changed.

And for the first time, I began to wonder if I had been wrong about everything.

A Moment That Changed Everything

She came over that afternoon, just like she always had. The sun was beginning its slow descent, casting warm streaks of gold through my window, and for a moment, everything felt like it used to. Comfortable. Familiar.

Joyce sat down in my room, her expression unreadable. And then, in a quiet voice, she said, "I have something to tell you."

I barely heard her. Or maybe, I didn't want to.

Instead, I reached for my guitar, eager to share something with her—something beautiful, something ours. I had spent weeks learning a new song, picturing the moment I'd play it for her. And now, here she was. Back from the blur of my time away at school, back in the one place where things made sense.

"Hold that thought," I told her, smiling.

Then, I began to play Too Much Heaven by the Bee Gees. The chords drifted softly between us, and in that moment, nothing else mattered. I was just a boy with a guitar, playing for a girl who had always been there.

Except, as the last note faded into the air, reality set in.

Joyce shifted in her seat, took a breath, and spoke the words that would change everything.

"I'm seeing someone... uh, he's a university guy."

At first, I thought I had misheard her.

I froze, my fingers still resting on the strings. My mind tried to make sense of it, but the words clashed against everything I had believed about us.

She wasn't mine. Not really. Not officially. But in my heart, she had always been the one I could return to. The one constant in a world that kept changing.

And now, she belonged to someone else.

It wasn't just any guy—it was a university guy. Older. Wiser. Someone who, by some unfair twist of fate, was also my older brother's friend.

I sat there in silence, swallowing down emotions I didn't even have names for yet. And when I found out later that she and this new guy had been coming over to my house—had been here, in my space, laughing with my brother while I was away—something inside me broke.

It wasn't just jealousy. It wasn't even heartbreak, not exactly. It was the ache of losing something I had never truly had.

For weeks, I walked around with that weight on my chest, not knowing what to do with it. The feeling of loss was new to me, raw and relentless, and no one had ever warned me how much it would hurt.

But in that pain, something shifted.

For the first time, I understood what it meant to truly care for someone—to want them to be yours, and to know you had to tell them before it was too late.

I realized that love, or whatever fragile thing I had been holding onto, wasn't just about expectation. It was about effort. About making someone a priority, about saying the words out loud instead of just assuming they already knew.

And perhaps the hardest lesson of all: if you don't claim your place in someone's heart, someone else will.

That summer, as I sat alone in my room, my guitar silent in my lap, I promised myself one thing.

Next time, I wouldn't leave things unspoken.

The Lessons of the Heart

I thought that with time, things would become clearer—that with every new experience, I'd come to understand girls and what they wanted, or at the very least, how they felt about me. But instead, I only found myself more confused.

The disappointment of losing Joyce had left a lingering emptiness, one I wasn't sure how to fill. Maybe I had been too naive, too focused on the idea of companionship without truly grasping what it meant to hold someone's heart. Maybe, I thought, if I had been more physical, things would have turned out differently. And yet, strangely, I never found myself daydreaming about sex. What I longed for was something else— the warmth of sitting beside a girl, the ease of conversation, the intoxicating thrill of simply being seen.

It became a quiet obsession of mine—figuring out which girls in the neighborhood I could get to know, who might share those moments with me. That was how I met Femi and Yaa.

They weren't just any girls—they were strikingly similar, enough that I wondered if I had unconsciously developed a preference. Maybe it was their smiles, or the way they laughed at my jokes, or simply the fact that they were willing to spend time with me. Whatever it was, I enjoyed their company. The late-night talks, the stolen moments in the park—it was enough for me to call them my girlfriends, even if nothing had been made official.

Femi was different, though. She was the youngest daughter of Baker Forson, the man who supplied bread to our house every morning. Because of that, I saw her often. Sometimes, she even came by to deliver the bread herself. She fascinated me in a way no other girl had. She was effortlessly charming, and I loved how easy it was to talk to her. Those nights we spent together, watching TV, snacking, laughing—it felt like something real, something I could hold on to.

Until the night that changed everything.

My mother had sent me out on an errand, nothing out of the ordinary. But as I returned home, my eyes caught a silhouette behind the wall near our house gates—two figures, pressed closely together. At first, I wasn't sure what I was seeing. But as I stepped closer, the truth hit me like a brick.

Femi.

My Femi.

Kissing my older brother.

My heart dropped. My stomach twisted. I ran, slamming the door behind me, locking myself away from the world. I didn't cry—I couldn't. I just sat there, drowning in a mixture of anger and humiliation. How could she? How could he?

That night, something in me hardened. I realized, painfully, that talking to a girl, spending time with her, even sharing laughter and secrets—none of it meant she was mine. If I wanted a girl to be mine, I had to make sure everyone knew it.

So I turned to Yaa.

She had always been easy to talk to, always eager to sneak away with me to the park. And now, she was my next move. I couldn't afford another loss. This time, I would make sure no other boy— no brother—would take her from me.

I enlisted the help of a friend my age, someone who could keep watch while I finally claimed what was supposed to be mine. He was to bring Yaa to my room and stand guard while I… figured things out.

When she walked in, I locked the door behind her. My heart pounded. She sat on my bed, looking at me expectantly. I hesitated for only a moment before reaching for her legs, letting my hands trail up her dress.

But then, she looked at me. Not in fear, not in excitement—just a straight, unreadable stare.

And I faltered.

My hands dropped. Embarrassment burned through me, and I turned away, ashamed of what I had been trying to force.

But then, to my utter shock, she took my hands.

"Lie down," she whispered.

My pulse roared in my ears. She guided me, instructed me, taking control in a way I had never imagined. It was overwhelming, exhilarating, terrifying all at once. I was schooled in ways I hadn't expected, my heart racing as she took my hand, ready to lead me further—

Then, from outside the room, a frantic voice.

"Come out, now!"

No. No, no, no. Not now.

My friend, the one standing guard, had betrayed us. Yaa's family had been looking for her, and someone had told her mother she was at my house.

Panic set in. We scrambled, dressing as fast as humanly possible. And then, without thinking, we did the only thing we could—we jumped out of the window.

Yaa ran home, slipping through the night before her mother stormed through my door, finding nothing but empty air.

I should have been relieved. I should have laughed it off as just another close call. But in the days that followed, something unexpected happened.

Yaa started telling everyone we were together.

That she was my girlfriend.

The irony of it all hit me hard. I had wanted to claim her—to make sure no one else did. But now, it was she who had claimed me. And the strangest part? Nothing had even happened.

But I learned something that day.

If you touch a girl—even if it's nothing, even if it means nothing—you take on the emotional weight of that moment. You own it, whether you meant to or not.

And maybe, just maybe, I was finally beginning to understand the gravity of what it meant to be with someone.

The Weight of Understanding

I thought back to Mia. To the way she had looked at me that Christmas Eve, more mature than I had ever realized, more aware of the emotional responsibility between a boy and a girl than I had been at the time.

She hadn't been coy about what she wanted. She had spelled it out plainly, first in person and then in a letter—one that, in its carefully chosen words, stripped away the mystery of what it meant to be with someone. Not just as a passing companion, not as a casual flirtation, but as a boyfriend in the truest sense of the word.

I could still remember reading her words, the way they forced me to confront something I had barely begun to grasp. She wasn't asking for a confession of love or empty promises; she wanted something real, something physical, and she had been waiting for me to make a move. My hesitation had pushed her to take the lead, to tell me outright what she had been hoping for.

And yet, even with all the clarity her letter had given me, that night never unfolded the way it could have.

We sat together for hours, the air between us heavy with expectation. She was there, right in front of me, giving me a moment I could have stepped into, a moment that could have changed everything.

But I didn't.

Not because I didn't want to. Not because I didn't care. But because a part of me—some deep, uncertain part—still didn't know how.

I had spent so much time caught up in the idea of love, of romance, of the thrill of simply being around a girl, that when faced with the reality of it, I hesitated. And that hesitation was something I had never been able to fully explain—not to Mia, not to myself.

Maybe it was fear. Maybe it was naivety. Or maybe it was something much older, something buried in my past that had shaped the way I viewed intimacy without me even realizing it.

Because the truth was, I had seen something once. Something I wasn't supposed to see.

It was years ago, in Dunkwah. I was just a boy, no older than eight. I had come home one afternoon, the air thick with heat, the house quiet except for the muffled sound of crying. At first, I thought I had imagined it. But as I followed the sound, it led me to the room of Mr. Last, a tenant who had rented from my parents.

His door was locked, but there was a keyhole.

Curiosity had made me press my eye against it, and what I saw on the other side made my stomach twist.

Mr. Last was on top of a woman, striking her as she sobbed beneath him.

50

I didn't understand what I was looking at, not fully. But I knew it was wrong. That much, even my eight-year-old mind could comprehend.

Panicked, I had run to my mother, breathless, trying to tell her what I had seen. But instead of outrage, instead of action, she had simply told me to mind my own business.

"Don't peep into people's rooms," she had said.

And just like that, the moment was dismissed. The woman's cries were ignored. And I was left with a lingering confusion that followed me into my teenage years, into my relationships, into every moment where I had the chance to be with a girl and hesitated.

Because if that was intimacy, if that was what men did to women behind closed doors, then I wanted no part of it.

I wasn't raised to be like Mr. Last. I refused to be like him.

And so, as much as I had wanted to understand what it meant to be with a girl beyond stolen moments and innocent touches, I held back. There was a part of me that needed to understand it on my own terms, that refused to rush into something I didn't fully comprehend.

But that didn't mean I wasn't curious.

After my experience with Yaa, something had shifted in me. The idea of intimacy—the intrigue of it, the pull of it—became something I thought about constantly. Not in a way that made me desperate to act on it, but in a way that fueled my imagination.

I found that I was better at fantasizing about intimacy than actually pursuing it. It felt safer that way—like a dream I could control, without the fear of doing something wrong, without the risk of exposing just how little I knew.

And so, instead of chasing experiences, I chased beauty. I let myself admire every girl who caught my eye, convinced that one day, I'd figure it all out.

One day, I'd understand what Mia had tried to teach me. What her letter had spelled out so clearly.

And maybe, when that day came, I wouldn't hesitate.

Running for My Life

I can't quite recall how I met Yaa G, but I will never forget how she made me feel. Like I was walking on air. Like I had stumbled into the kind of moment that songs and poems were made of. When she invited me over one evening, it felt like a golden ticket—an invitation into a world where, for once, I wasn't just another boy chasing after the idea of love. This time, I was chosen.

But given my history of not exactly sticking around when things got complicated with girls, I decided to play it safe. I brought my best friend, Moon Tiger.

Moon Tiger was more than just a friend—he was my accomplice in everything that mattered. We spent endless hours dissecting the mysteries of the universe, or at least, the mysteries of women. So when I told him about Yaa G, he didn't hesitate to come along. As luck would have it, he already knew her. That was enough to convince me that this night, if nothing else, would be interesting.

It was a crisp Friday evening, the kind where the air hums with possibility. When we arrived at her house, she greeted us with a smile that could make time stop. Effortless. Magnetic. The kind of smile that makes a guy believe in fate. She led us upstairs to the family's living room, moving with a confidence that made my pulse quicken.

And then there were her pajamas.

Silk. Delicate. Clinging to her like moonlight. It wasn't even that late, but neither Moon Tiger nor I dared to question it. We were too caught up in the magic of it all, too grateful for this unexpected glimpse into her world.

But magic has a way of turning into disaster when you least expect it.

The living room door burst open with the force of a thunderclap. My heart nearly stopped. For a split second, I thought maybe the wind had hurled a tree branch straight through it.

But no.

It was something far more terrifying.

A towering figure stood in the doorway, his shadow swallowing the room whole. Her father.

His voice boomed like an earthquake.

"Who the hell are you?"

The room went still. My body refused to move. My mouth went dry.

Yaa G, to her credit, remained composed. But her father wasn't looking for explanations. He was looking for us to disappear.

"Get the hell out of my house!"

And just like that, the spell was broken.

There was no room for negotiation. No time for clever excuses. Just the raw, primal instinct to run. And run we did.

I had spent my life running from girls. But that night, I ran for my life.

Front Doors and Back Doors

Her father was no different than mine.

My father, too, had rules.

Girls did not belong in the house—not in our rooms, not behind closed doors. It didn't matter how innocent it was. He didn't care about what was said between a boy and a girl. He only cared that they were alone, and to him, that was enough to be a problem.

He usually came home around 6:30 p.m., so any girl who dared to visit knew to be gone by six. It was an unspoken rule, a curfew written into the fabric of my teenage years.

But one day, a girl stayed too long.

We were in the boys' quarters, listening to music, the sound of the speakers drowning out the ticking clock. We lost track of time—until there was a knock on the door.

I knew, before I even opened it, that my time had run out.

My father stood there, silent but commanding. "See the girl off and come inside," he said.

That was it. That was all.

I knew what was coming next.

Standing before my mother, he issued the decree: No more girls in the house. Ever.

And just like that, the front doors were closed to me.

But here's the thing about being young—closed doors don't stop you. They just make you smarter.

Where front doors were denied to me, back doors became the new path. There were always ways around the rules. Ways to sneak, to hide, to slip through the cracks without being caught.

There was a thrill in it, in the secrecy, in the whispered plans and stolen moments. We lied. We hid. We took risks because we had to.

And maybe, deep down, I knew this was how it had always been. I had read enough love stories—Romeo and Juliet, forbidden romances woven into history—to understand that some things had to be lived. Some experiences had to be chased, no matter the consequences, if only to prove to myself that my youth wasn't slipping through my fingers.

Maybe I wasn't ready for love. Maybe I still didn't fully understand what it meant to be with someone.

But I knew, without a doubt, that I wasn't going to let anyone—not my father, not her father, not the rules of the world—stop me from trying to find out.

The Forbidden Fruit

After that harrowing escape from Akosua G's house, I should have taken it as a sign to stay away. But the opposite happened.

She became more attractive to me.

Maybe it was ego—some primal need to prove that I could have what had been snatched away from me. Or maybe it was the sheer thrill of it, the way danger always seems to add an irresistible edge to desire. Whatever it was, I wanted her. Not just in passing, not just as another fleeting infatuation, but in a way that burned itself into my memory.

It has been almost thirty-five years, yet I can still see her as if it were yesterday—standing there in her golden kimono pajamas, the silk draping over her body in a way that made it impossible to look away. The way the fabric clung to her curves, how she moved so effortlessly, completely unaware of the power she had in that moment. That night cemented something in me. I wasn't just thinking about any girl—I was thinking about her.

I watched for my chance, and one summer night, it finally came.

It was warm, the kind of night where the air felt thick with possibility. Akosua G came to my house, and somehow, we found ourselves alone. There was no rush this time, no thunderous interruption. Just the two of us, kissing, exploring, giving in to the weight of everything that had been building between us.

And then, just as we reached the point where there was no turning back, she panicked. And I… I got scared too.

We stopped. We agreed to stop.

Maybe it was fear. Maybe it was the unknown. But that moment taught me something—I wasn't ready, and neither was she.

Afterward, as we sat in the quiet aftermath of what almost was, she looked at me and asked a question that caught me completely off guard.

"Are we boyfriend and girlfriend now?"

I froze.

I had never been asked that so directly before. In all my encounters, in all the moments I had spent dreaming about being close to a girl, I had never considered this. The after.

Because to me, this had been about the experience. About curiosity, about knowing what it felt like to make out, to touch, to explore. But I hadn't thought about what came next.

The truth was, I didn't know what being a boyfriend really meant.

Was that what this was? Did physical closeness automatically translate into something deeper, something more binding?

I didn't know how to answer her, so I didn't. Not in the way she probably wanted. Instead, I let the moment slip away, let the silence speak for me.

And, in time, I moved on.

Because how could I limit myself to just one girl? There were so many—beautiful, different, each with something unique to offer. The world felt too vast, too full of possibility, to confine myself to just one experience, one person.

But looking back, I know now what I didn't understand then— she wasn't just asking a question. She was asking for certainty. She was asking me to define something she had already decided for herself.

And I had failed to do so.

A Private Search

The years that followed were a time of quiet rebellion. I knew what I wanted to explore, and I also knew that it was forbidden.

My parents had never explicitly told me why. They didn't sit me down and explain the consequences of desire or the weight of emotional responsibility. They only made it clear—through their rules, their expectations, their unspoken warnings—that certain things were out of bounds.

And I knew, without a doubt, that if I ever got caught, there would be consequences.

So I searched for experiences in secret.

Not out of defiance, but out of need.

I wanted to understand, to figure out this uncharted territory without someone dictating the rules to me. And in that quiet pursuit, I discovered something about myself—something both thrilling and terrifying.

I was better at wanting intimacy than actually engaging in it.

I could fantasize endlessly—about touch, about love, about what it might mean to truly be with someone—but when it came to actually crossing the line, I always hesitated. Maybe it was fear of getting caught. Maybe it was fear of the unknown. Or maybe it was something deeper, something I hadn't yet learned to name.

But one thing was certain.

I wasn't going to stop searching.

OHENE AKU KWAPONG

4

Fly Me to the Moon

Love—it's the one thing we all search for, the one thing we all need. It starts in childhood, wrapped in the warmth of our parents' arms, in the quiet reassurance of their presence. But as we grow, life nudges us forward, steering us toward new kinds of love, toward the kind that comes with companionship, shared dreams, and whispered secrets in the dark.

For me, love has always been about finding that one woman— the one who makes the world feel whole, who turns the ordinary into something extraordinary. As a boy, my experiences with girls were simple, playful, and filled with innocent mischief. We laughed, we explored the uncharted waters of young attraction, and in our own way, we had each other's backs. But looking back, I realize now how little I truly understood.

There was a time when I thought love was just about spending time together—holding hands, stealing glances across a crowded room, sharing dances under the stars. But love, I would learn, is more than that. It's about presence, about truly seeing someone and making them feel like the center of your universe, even if just for a moment.

Mia's letter changed everything for me. It was in her words that I glimpsed a truth I had never fully grasped—girls wanted to be treasured, to be adored, to feel like they were the most precious thing in the world to the person they gave their heart to. And for all my well-intended gestures, I had never truly understood that before.

I struggled with the emotional language of love, the unspoken expectations that existed beyond the surface. There were moments of clarity, of course, but they were fleeting—like trying to hold water in my hands. I was too young, too naive to see what was right in front of me. One girl, much later in life, summed it up perfectly with a sharp-edged truth: If I'm going to cry over you being late, I'd rather do it in a BMW than on a bicycle. Love, it seemed, was never just about the heart—it was tangled up in reality, in the choices we made, in the kind of future we could offer.

Most of the time, I simply didn't know what was expected of me. And when I did, it was because someone had to spell it out. Women, I've come to learn, possess a certain knowing—a kind of instinct that allows them to see beyond words, beyond actions, into the very core of a moment. Me? I was blind to it. I had always been.

I remember sitting with my brother once, voicing my frustration over this very thing—how love felt like a language I couldn't quite learn, no matter how hard I tried. He looked at me, smiled in that knowing way older brothers do, and said, You have to learn how to make soup with meat. At first, it meant nothing. But later, as life unfolded in its quiet, relentless way, I understood.

Love isn't about having all the answers. It's about learning the recipe, about understanding the ingredients that make something beautiful, something worth holding on to. And for the first time in my life, I wanted to learn. I wanted to get it right.

Life has a way of teaching us lessons when we least expect them, often in the form of people who cross our paths, even if just for a moment. My older brother was one of those guiding lights, his wisdom slipping into my life at just the right moments, helping me navigate the complicated, often bewildering world of relationships. But there were some lessons I had to learn on my own.

MIT was a world unlike any I had known. It was a coed college, filled with brilliant minds from every corner of the world, and for a seventeen-year-old boy fresh from my home country, it was an overwhelming sea of fast-talking, quick-thinking people. The American accent alone was a challenge—I found myself asking people to slow down, struggling to catch the rhythm of their words, let alone the slang that peppered their conversations. I spent nights watching news broadcasts and movies, training my ear, trying to fit in.

Althea was the first friend I made on campus. She was curious about where I was from, about the life I had left behind, and I found myself opening up to her in a way I hadn't expected. She was easy to talk to, easy to be around. One night, she invited me to dinner at her dorm. I had agreed—only to completely forget about it. As it turned out, that forgetfulness had been a blessing, because her dorm was strictly for girls. The next day, she gave me that look, the one that said she had been waiting, but she never held it against me. We stayed close, studying together, sharing thoughts on life and everything in between. And yet, for all our friendship, I knew there was something different about this connection. She wasn't just another girl I could joke around with like one of the guys. She was purposeful, intentional. And that scared me.

Then there was Amy.

I met her at a party at Wellesley College, a girls' school about forty miles from Boston. That night, she was the one who came to me. She asked me to dance, and without hesitation, I took her hand. It was effortless, the way we moved together, the way the night seemed to fold around us as if we were the only two people in the room. We held each other close, our hands finding their natural places, our bodies in sync with the music. It was the first time I felt no fear in the presence of a girl who was interested in me.

Several times, she whispered that we should step outside for some air, but I resisted, lost in the rhythm of the dance, in the warmth of her touch. I must have worn her out, keeping her on the dance floor for hours. Finally, she insisted, and we found ourselves outside, breathing in the cool night air, our fingers still loosely laced together.

That was when she told me she liked me.

The words were simple, yet they carried weight, an invitation I wasn't ready for. She spoke of her new dorm, the place she had moved into, and how her old room—now empty—was just a short walk away. Did I want to see it?

Clueless. That's what I was. Instead of recognizing what she was offering, I blurted out that I would love for us to be pen pals. Pen pals. As if this was some innocent, schoolyard friendship. I went on and on about how wonderful it would be to exchange letters, to write about our days and our thoughts.

That was the last time I ever saw her.

Months later, I pieced together what I had been too blind to see that night. I had missed it—the moment, the connection, the possibility of something real. No third-party introductions, no games. Just a girl who had chosen me. And I had let her slip away.

That night changed something in me. It made me realize that when a girl knows what she wants, she doesn't waste time. There are no riddles, no hidden meanings—just truth, raw and direct. And if a man is too slow to catch it, too blind to see what's right in front of him, he'll lose his chance.

By my second year, I had vowed never to let that happen again. I pursued the girls I liked with the urgency of someone who had learned that opportunities in love don't wait. Like a pendulum swinging in the opposite direction, I went after what I wanted, unafraid, unwilling to let fate dictate what was now in my own hands.

Some nights are ordinary, slipping by unnoticed in the quiet hum of routine. And then there are nights when fate decides to rewrite your story.

The international students' party was supposed to be just that—a party. I had no expectations, no hopes beyond the music and the easy camaraderie of people who, like me, were trying to find their place in a world far from home. But as if Providence had finally decided to grant me a second chance, she appeared.

Her name was India. She was French, confident, and as effortlessly alluring as the country she came from. She walked up to me, her eyes holding a kind of knowing amusement, and asked me to dance.

This time, I was ready. I played it differently, pretending I wasn't much of a dancer, letting conversation take the lead instead of the music. We talked for hours, the rhythm of our words replacing the beat of the songs around us. By the end of the night, we exchanged phone numbers, and before I even left, I had already set up our first date. I told myself this was my moment—my chance to make up for what I had lost with Amy.

The next evening, we met at a small Chinese restaurant near her place. I let her choose it, wanting her to feel at ease, wanting to get everything right this time. The food was good, but the company was better. By the time we finished, I had my leftovers boxed up, and as we walked out, she asked if I wanted to leave them at her place before the movie so I could pick them up later.

I said yes before she could even finish the sentence.

A few minutes later, I found myself standing in her apartment, wedging my takeout box into a tight spot in her fridge. I don't remember what movie we watched that night—I doubt I even registered a single scene. What I do remember is India. The way her denim jeans fit her just right, the soft sway of her pleated brown blouse, the way her faded denim jacket made her seem effortlessly cool. And most of all, I remember the single thought running through my mind the entire time: my fried rice was my ticket back to her apartment.

When the movie ended, we returned to her place, under the pretense of picking up my food. But once inside, we sank onto her sofa, the conversation flowing easily, comfortably, until it wasn't so easy anymore. Until she turned to me with those sharp, searching eyes and asked me a question I wasn't prepared for.

"Do you like me?"

"Of course I do," I replied without hesitation.

She studied me for a moment before asking again. "Are you sure?"

"Yes," I said, meaning it. But I hadn't yet learned that in matters of the heart, meaning something wasn't always enough.

Then I made a mistake. A classic, world-shifting, foot-in-mouth mistake.

"I like a lot of people."

Her expression changed. "What do you mean you like a lot of people?"

I tried to explain—poorly—that back home in Ghana, liking someone wasn't such an exclusive thing. That I liked Althea too, and plenty of other people. I thought I was clarifying. Instead, I was digging myself into a hole so deep I might never have climbed out of it.

And then came the question that unraveled everything.

"What do you want from me, then?"

I didn't think. I answered the only way that felt true.

"I want you."

India went completely still. "You know what you're saying, right?"

It was only then that I realized we were not speaking the same language—not really. The words were the same, but their meanings were oceans apart. I had meant it simply, the way I would have back home. But here, in this foreign land with its unfamiliar rules of love and courtship, those three words meant something else entirely.

Her frustration faded into amusement as she realized I truly had no clue what I had just said. Patiently, she explained the nuances of American slang, how liking someone meant attraction, but wanting someone... well, that meant something far more intimate. And then, as if to test me one final time, she asked again.

"Do you want me?"

I looked at her, really looked at her. And this time, I knew exactly what I was saying.

"Yes."

That night, India became more than just another lesson in my journey of understanding women. She became the moment everything changed—the moment I learned, not just about language, but about intimacy, about connection, about the unspoken desires that draw two people together.

That night, I didn't just step into a new world. I let it consume me. And India? She became my first real girlfriend.

If you've ever truly listened to the lyrics of Fly Me to the Moon, you'd know that love—real love—takes you beyond what you thought was possible. It carries you to places you never knew existed, and even when you think you understand it, you realize you don't. That was how I felt in those first years in America, especially after that unforgettable night with India.

It wasn't just about love; it was about understanding, about learning how to communicate in a world that spoke a language I thought I knew—but didn't. The night with India had been a wake-up call. I didn't just need to learn how to talk; I needed to learn how to listen, how to understand the weight behind words.

The very next day, determined to never misinterpret another moment, I went to the English Department at MIT and asked to see a professor. When they asked why, I simply said, It's personal.

That was how I met Cathy Higgins.

Cathy was more than just a professor; she became my lifeline in those early years. Every Saturday, I sat in her office as she broke down the language—not just the words, but the rhythm, the phrases, the nuances that made American English feel like a completely different dialect from the one I had studied. She taught me how the jaw moves when speaking, how intonations shift meanings, and how idioms could turn an innocent sentence into something completely different. I would have been lost without her.

With time, my confidence grew. India and I grew closer, and for the next two years, we built a romance that taught me what it meant to truly be with someone. But even with India, even with everything I had learned, I still felt there was more to understand about women, about relationships, about love itself.

And then came Vanessa.

I met her at a birthday party, and from the very start, it was fireworks—not the kind that burns fast and fizzles out, but the kind that lights up the sky, leaving you in awe. We argued the entire night, moving from one heated debate to another, our words crashing into each other like waves against a cliff. Even the party hosts were stunned by our energy.

Vanessa wasn't just opinionated—she was brilliant. I later found out she was studying law at Tufts University, not government as I had assumed. She was sharp, quick-witted, and she laughed in a way that stayed with you long after she was gone.

When the night ended, she looked at me and said, I'd like to take you out when I get back from D.C.

There was no hesitation, no waiting for me to make the first move—just pure, confident intention. That was what pulled me in.

When she returned, we met up, and for the first time, I saw her dressed up, polished in a way that made me do a double take. She was stunning. That night, we talked about everything—our childhoods, our dreams, the ridiculousness of life. We laughed, hopping from one bar to another, dancing, drinking, living.

The night ended at Ahmed's, a nightclub in the heart of Harvard Square, a place unlike anything I had ever seen—where black men and white women filled the room, mingling, moving, blurring whatever social lines were meant to exist. But for Vanessa and me, it was just another stop on a night that felt infinite. We were from different worlds—me from Africa, her from England—what did we know of America's contradictions?

At 1:00 a.m., I put her in a taxi and rode with her back to her dorm. As I turned to leave, she grabbed me, her fingers tightening around my wrist.

"You almost made me kill you that first night," she whispered, her voice half-playful, half-serious. "But tonight, I think I've fallen in love."

And just like that, I was gone.

Vanessa was unlike any woman I had ever known. She was bold, unafraid, and she changed my entire idea of what love could be. That night, for the first time in my life, I spent the night with a woman. And it wasn't just about passion—it was about feeling safe, about knowing I was with someone who saw me completely and still wanted to stay.

For three years, we built a life together. I graduated and moved to New York, and when she finished school, she followed. We created a rhythm of our own—arguing, laughing, playing, even having pillow fights like two kids who had stumbled into love by accident.

"If we don't get married," I used to tell her, "I'll have to find someone else I can have pillow fights with."

That was Vanessa and me—an undeniable force, two people who could challenge each other and still find their way back to laughter.

One night, before she moved to New York, I visited her in Brooklyn before a big exam. She was at the library, so I let myself into her apartment and cooked her dinner before slipping out without saying a word. She was furious at first that I hadn't stayed the night. But when she finally came to New York, she wrapped her arms around me and kissed me, whispering thank you against my lips. She had needed to study, and I had known that—even when she hadn't.

That was Vanessa—fiery, beautiful, unforgettable. She left a mark on me, one I carry even now.

Love, I had learned, wasn't about perfection. It wasn't about always knowing the right thing to say or do. It was about being present, about learning, about letting yourself be vulnerable enough to grow with someone. And with Vanessa, I had done just that.

She was the first woman to truly leave an imprint on my life. And I like to believe I left one on hers too.

There are certain truths a man only comes to understand after he has truly lived, after he has loved and lost, after he has found himself utterly undone by the presence of a woman.

For me, it took time. It took moments of fumbling cluelessness, of missed opportunities, of learning the language of love the hard way. But with each experience—with India, with Vanessa, with all the women who had walked into my life, even for just a brief moment—I began to understand something profound.

Women shape the world.

They are the source of its color, its texture, its rhythm. Without them, I imagine life would be dry, tasteless—a hollow melody without lyrics, a story without characters worth remembering. Love, passion, even the way we push ourselves to become better men—so much of it, whether we admit it or not, is tied to them.

I had spent so much of my youth curious about women, trying to figure them out, trying to navigate the mystery of what they wanted and how to give it to them. But now, I saw things differently. It wasn't just about attraction, about learning the right words or making the right moves. It was about appreciating them for what they were—the heart of everything, the force that made life not just bearable, but extraordinary.

They were the reason men stayed up at night, writing poetry they'd never share. The reason songs were written, wars were fought, and history was made. They were the reason for whispered conversations between friends, for secrets shared over late-night drinks, for the ache in a man's chest when he realizes he's let the right one slip away.

And I, in my own way, was beginning to understand that.

Women were not just companions, not just lovers. They were muses, they were challengers, they were the quiet strength behind every great story. And in my life, they had already begun shaping me into the man I was becoming.

The journey wasn't over yet. There was still more to learn, still more to feel, still more love to experience.

But one thing was certain—I would never take them for granted again.

Chapter 5

She Scares the Hell Out of Me

There are moments in life that change you forever—moments so breathtakingly beautiful that you wish they could last a lifetime, and others so unsettling that they shake you to your core. My time with Vanessa was a little bit of both.

She was the kind of woman who could make you believe in love the way it's written in books—effortless, full of laughter, the kind where you find yourself smiling for no reason at all. We fit together in a way I thought only happened in the movies, two people looking out for each other, making the world a little softer just by being in it together. I did everything I could to make her happy, and for a while, I thought that was enough. But life, as it so often does, had other plans.

Vanessa smoked. At first, it was just another part of her, something that didn't seem important in the grand scheme of things. But as the years passed, my worry grew. Maybe it was irrational, maybe it was just fear gnawing at the edges of my contentment, but I couldn't ignore it. I brought it up more than I should have, and each time, she pulled away just a little more. To her, it was a choice—one that she wasn't willing to reconsider, no matter how much I pleaded. And that terrified me.

Because if she couldn't change this—if she couldn't even see why I was so afraid—what else wouldn't she change? What if, one day, something bigger came along, something we couldn't fix, and she turned away just as easily?

It reminded me of Jennifer.

I had met her in Boston, back when I was still trying to figure out who I was. She was a part of a sorority at Wellesley, while I was wrapped up in the whirlwind of MIT and the International Students Club. Our relationship had been easy in the way young love often is—long walks, late-night conversations, promises whispered between kisses. And then, one September afternoon, everything changed.

The phone rang, and the moment I answered, I knew something was wrong.

"Who the hell do you think you are?" a woman's voice lashed out at me, sharp and furious. Before I could respond, she pressed on, her words laced with accusation. "Do you love my daughter?"

The question took me by surprise. "Yes," I said, my stomach tightening.

She wasn't satisfied. "Do you love her enough to marry her?"

The world tilted. "What?"

I nearly dropped the phone. My heart pounded as I tried to make sense of what was happening. I asked to speak to Jennifer, but instead, her brother took the phone.

"I'm going to break your neck," he seethed, "because you got my sister pregnant."

The words barely registered. Pregnant? Jennifer? My mind raced, my thoughts colliding in a panic. When they finally let me talk to her, she confirmed it. She was pregnant, and I was the father.

Everything after that was a blur of fear and responsibility. I told her I'd come down after my exams to meet her family, to make things right. But she refused. There was hesitation in her voice, something unspoken, something I didn't understand—until the next morning when she called again.

I wasn't the only one she had been seeing.

The truth unraveled like a cruel joke. The baby wasn't mine. She had used my name because I was at MIT, while the other guy— the real father—was someone her family wouldn't accept. She had broken down after our conversation, confessing everything to her parents, and in the end, I was spared. I was out of the picture.

But I wasn't untouched.

That phone call changed me. It made me realize just how fragile everything was, how one moment, one choice, could alter my life forever.

Vanessa had no idea about Jennifer. I never told her. But when she refused to change, when she dismissed my fears as nothing more than nagging, I felt that same dread creeping in—the same helplessness, the same gut-wrenching realization that I was standing on the edge of something I couldn't control.

And that scared the hell out of me.

A Leap of Faith

Vanessa and I ended the way some love stories do—not with anger or betrayal, but with a quiet understanding that love alone isn't always enough. It wasn't a bitter breakup; it was a

75

realization. We had fought for each other, held on as long as we could, but in the end, it was our stubbornness—mine in wanting her to change, hers in refusing to—that finally pulled us apart.

After she left, New York felt impossibly vast. The city that had once felt like an adventure now felt like an echo chamber, its crowded streets doing nothing to drown out the silence she had left behind. Loneliness in a place like this is a strange thing—it follows you into subway cars and lingers in coffee shops, a constant companion even in a sea of people. But, as it turns out, loneliness has a way of leading you to unexpected places.

One evening, I met a group of students at Columbia who invited me to church. It was a new congregation, young, full of energy, and I figured, why not? Maybe a fresh start was exactly what I needed. What I didn't know then was that walking through those church doors would lead me into one of the most bewildering experiences of my life.

At first, it was great. The church emphasized friendships, encouraging us to meet as many people as possible, to form bonds before seeking anything deeper. It seemed harmless— refreshing, even. There was no pressure, no expectations, just a community. But in time, I realized something: the women weren't there for casual connections. They were looking for husbands. And I? I wasn't looking for anything at all.

The Church of Christ had about two thousand members, and for three years, I tried to navigate this unusual world of platonic dating, of getting to know multiple women with no clear direction. It was, in theory, an ideal setup—no obligations, no immediate commitment. But in practice? It was a minefield. No matter how well-intentioned, hearts were still fragile things, and without meaning to, I found myself hurting women who had expectations I couldn't fulfill.

In my second year at the church, I discovered that one of the women, Gabela, was a professor at Columbia, where I was a graduate student. She was intelligent, confident, and carried herself with a quiet grace. I admired that. So one afternoon, I walked into her office and, without much preamble, asked, "Ms. Gabela, would you like to go on a date with me?"

She laughed. Loudly.

Not exactly the response I was hoping for.

When she saw that I was serious, her amusement faded into surprise. "But I'm a professor," she said, as if that explained everything.

I shrugged. "And we go to the same church," I countered. "Besides, I happen to like smart women."

She didn't say no. Instead, she asked for time to think about it, and I left her office feeling a strange mix of exhilaration and panic. I had just asked a professor out. What was I thinking?

Days passed with no word from her. Then, on Sunday, I found out—from someone else—that she had shared my proposition with a mutual friend.

I stood there, stunned.

It wasn't that I blamed her for hesitating. I understood the risks, the hesitations, the boundaries that a professor-student dynamic created. But she could have told me that herself. Instead, she had taken my request and turned it into a topic of conversation, discussing me with others before giving me an answer.

That Wednesday, I saw her at a church event, but neither of us spoke. Later that night, a friend called to tell me that she had finally agreed to go out with me.

But by then, it didn't matter.

I should have been happy, relieved even, but all I felt was disappointment. It wasn't her hesitation that stung—it was the way she had handled it, the way she had made me feel like a subject of curiosity rather than a man worthy of an answer. And if that was how things started, then maybe it was better they never started at all.

So I let it go.

Somewhere in another world, in another life, maybe things would have been different. Maybe we would have had a love story worth telling. But in this one?

It was never meant to be.

The Weight of Expectations

It was late, and the hum of fluorescent lights in the lab did little to keep my exhaustion at bay. I had buried myself in work, trying to push past the lingering irritation I still felt about Gabela. Then came a knock at the door.

I turned, and there she was.

She hesitated for a moment before stepping inside, her expression softer than I'd ever seen it. "I wanted to apologize," she said, her voice quieter than usual. "I was freaked out by your request. You're a student, and I'm a professor. That's not the norm."

There was something about the way she said it, the way she reached for my hand, that made the anger I had been holding onto dissolve. I could see it now—her hesitation wasn't meant to belittle me. It was fear, uncertainty. And I understood that.

So I forgave her.

We planned our first date soon after, something simple but intimate. My apartment, a home-cooked meal, music drifting softly in the background, conversation that lasted far longer than I expected. My roommate and her roommate were there, making it feel less like a traditional date and more like an evening among friends. But there was something in the way she looked at me, something in the way she laughed at my jokes, that made it clear—this was the beginning of something.

At the end of the night, I insisted on taking her home. I regret that decision to this day.

She lived two hours away. I didn't have a car, so we took the train together, then walked another thirty minutes to her house from the station. By the time I got back to my apartment, it was well past 3:00 a.m. The exhaustion was real, but so was the exhilaration.

The next day, she surprised me. She walked up to me on campus and handed me a card.

Inside, she had written: You are one of the most impressive men I've ever met.

A professor saying that to me—a student—felt like validation I didn't even know I needed.

Over time, we grew closer. Mini-dates, long conversations, quiet moments that felt more meaningful than grand gestures. But as things deepened with Gabela, I also found myself meeting new people at church.

And then came Rachel.

She was visiting from Philadelphia, a friend of Gabela's, and something about her felt... easier. Unlike with Gabela, I didn't feel like I was constantly trying to prove something. With Rachel, I could just be.

We started dating, and while I liked her, I quickly noticed a pattern. She always wanted our dates to happen in Philadelphia. Not once did she suggest meeting in New York. And somehow, despite the inconvenience, I always said yes.

At the time, I didn't mind. I had just bought my first car—a black Volkswagen Jetta—and I took pride in the long drives, the hours on the road between New York and Philadelphia. But six months in, I looked at the odometer and realized I had put 60,000 miles on it.

Sixty. Thousand. Miles.

All for Rachel.

I wanted to believe we were building something, something that would last, something that wouldn't crumble like my past relationships had. But beneath the surface, a fear gnawed at me—that I was going to lose her, too, just like I lost Vanessa. And so, I did everything I could to make sure that wouldn't happen. I overcompensated. I poured energy into making things easy for her, into making her happy, hoping that if I gave enough, she would stay.

But something else dawned on me.

This wasn't just about Rachel. Or Vanessa. Or Gabela.

It was about the kind of women I kept falling for. Women who were fiercely independent, unshakable in who they were, unwilling to compromise the pieces of themselves that made them whole. And in every relationship, I found myself running into the same wall.

With Vanessa, it was her smoking—a habit I couldn't accept.

With Gabela, it was her constant need for assurance, something that wore me down.

With Rachel, it was her unwillingness to meet me halfway, her expectation that I would always be the one to make the effort.

It wasn't that they were wrong in who they were. It was that I struggled with the demands that came with loving them. Every relationship felt like a negotiation, a battle of wills, a tug-of-war between what they wanted and what I needed.

And I hated that.

I hated relationships where every conversation felt like a debate. Where instead of two people growing together, it became a checklist of demands—This is what I want. This is who I am. Take it or leave it.

Love shouldn't feel like a set of rules and ultimatums.

And maybe… maybe that was why, no matter how much I tried, I kept finding myself back at square one.

Lessons in Independence

Then came Irene.

She was different.

You know that feeling when you step outside after a long, stuffy day indoors, and the air feels crisp and new against your skin? That was Irene—an unexpected breath of fresh air, unburdened by expectations, by past hurts, by the need to negotiate the terms of love before it even began.

She was younger, full of life, and fiercely intelligent. A student at Columbia, dreaming of a future in medicine. We started as acquaintances, then friends, our conversations revolving around studies, research programs, the pressures of academia. And somewhere in those late-night discussions and shared moments of quiet understanding, I found myself drawn to her.

She left for Dartmouth to specialize in infectious diseases, and when she returned to New York, we picked up where we left off. But this time, it was different. I saw her in a new light. She was articulate, confident, and unaffected by the complications that seemed to define every other woman I had tried to love. I was beginning to like her—a lot.

But Irene? She wasn't interested in dating.

Not me. Not anyone.

She had tried the whole relationship thing before, she told me, and it never ended well. She had made peace with it, chosen a different path. Instead of romantic entanglements, she surrounded herself with male friends, men she could talk to, laugh with—without the weight of expectations pressing down on her.

And that's when I learned another important lesson.

Love wasn't about a man making a choice. It wasn't about persistence, about effort, about proving oneself worthy. The woman had to be equally invested, equally willing to take that leap of faith. Without that, no amount of effort could change the outcome.

It made me wonder—could I love someone who had already decided that love wasn't for her?

I thought back to all the women I had loved before. Vanessa, Rachel, Gabela. Strong, independent, brilliant in their own right. And yet, each of those relationships had felt like a battlefield. They came armed with their pasts, with their expectations, with the unspoken hurts of men who had come before me. And somehow, I always found myself caught in the crossfire.

With Rachel, it was the never-ending demands, the expectation that I would always be the one to make the effort.

With Gabela, it was the constant need for reassurance, the feeling that no matter how much I gave, it would never be enough.

With Vanessa, it was the simple but unwavering refusal to change something that was tearing us apart.

Dating them felt like sitting in a classroom, absorbing lessons I never asked for. Complaints, arguments, unresolved wounds from past relationships being projected onto me before I even had a chance to prove who I was.

I wanted to understand women, to truly see them, but what I saw often scared me. Because it wasn't just about love—it was about power, about control, about who was willing to compromise and who wasn't. And too often, it felt like I was walking into relationships where the terms had already been set, where I was simply being measured against an invisible checklist, built from the ghosts of relationships past.

But Irene?

She had no checklist. No demands. No expectations of who I needed to be.

And yet, that terrified me too.

Because how do you hold onto something when there's nothing tethering it to you?

I had spent so much time trying to make things work with women who challenged me, who debated and negotiated and pushed back at every turn. Now, here was Irene, uncomplicated, untangled from the weight of past heartbreaks, and I didn't know if I could handle it.

I admired independent women. I always had. Their confidence, their ambition, their unwillingness to shrink themselves for anyone. But I had also come to fear them, to brace myself for the inevitable tug-of-war, the push and pull of who had to bend first.

With Irene, there was no war.

And maybe that was the scariest thing of all.

6

The Man of My Life

Looking back, my approach to women and relationships felt reckless—like a man swinging a sword blindly, unaware of the damage he might cause. The good book describes an unmarried man in just such a way, and I was living proof of it. I had no real strategy, no real understanding of what I was doing, just trial and error, with a lot of mistakes in between. There had to be men out there who knew better—who approached relationships with wisdom, patience, and intention. And I needed one of them in my life.

I needed a man—not just as a friend, but as a guide, a mentor, someone to help me navigate the emotional labyrinth I kept finding myself lost in. Someone who could tell me when I was about to mess up, or better yet, help me see when I already had. Because with all the women I dated in New York City, I know I must have unintentionally hurt some of them. Not because I wanted to, but because I didn't know any better.

To all the women out there—if you meet a man and he doesn't have another, older man in his life to counsel him on how to treat a woman, RUN!

I learned that lesson the hard way.

While I was struggling to figure out my situation with Professor Gabela, I met Andrea. She was from Croatia, studying at Columbia's School of Architecture, and she was unlike any woman I had ever met before. Graceful. Wise beyond her years. Motherly, but not in a way that felt overbearing. She had a calming spirit, one that made me feel at ease in a way few others did.

Unlike the women I had dated before, Andrea never made our time together about her. She wasn't interested in testing me or pushing for something more. She just wanted to be there for me, to guide me in her quiet, steady way.

One day, she asked me to go shopping with her on Broadway. I didn't think much of it at first—just a casual outing. But as we walked from store to store, I realized she was trying to send me a message.

"You always wear green and brown," she said, picking up a pale blue shirt and holding it up to my chest. "You should try something different."

I hadn't given much thought to my clothes before. My wardrobe, now that I really thought about it, probably looked like something out of a Cuban revolution. But Andrea was kind about it. She never made me feel embarrassed. She just showed me what could be different—what could be better.

Eventually, she convinced me to buy a light pink shirt and a pair of blue jeans. Pink? Not my color. But she insisted.

That Sunday, I wore them to church.

The number of compliments I got was unbelievable.

That was Andrea's gift. She saw people, really saw them, and helped them become the best versions of themselves—not for her benefit, but for theirs. She never made it about her. She wanted me to shine.

She became like a sister to me. A trusted friend, someone I could talk to about the women I dated, someone who helped me make sense of my own feelings. And she was the one who introduced me to Arthur—the man who would become the man of my life.

Arthur was older, wiser, and exactly the influence I had been missing. With his guidance and Andrea's steady friendship, I finally started to reassess myself in the dating game. And I realized something: it was time to make a decision.

There were three women in my life, and I needed to choose.

But whoever I chose also had to choose me. That part was not lost on me.

The first was Rachel.

It was June 1989. She was throwing a house party in Philadelphia, and I drove down from New York to be there. I had spent the whole day on campus, barely had time to breathe before getting behind the wheel for the three-hour drive, but I made it.

Rachel met me at the party, introduced me to her friends. One of them, Mike—who I considered my inside man, someone who kept an eye out for any competition in Rachel's life—offered me his room to freshen up.

I took him up on the offer.

And then, to my own surprise, I fell asleep.

The party went on without me. Hours passed. I never made an appearance.

Rachel eventually came looking for me, only to find me fast asleep. She was furious.

"The party's almost over," she snapped. "And you've been in here sleeping?"

I sat up, rubbing my eyes. "I drove three hours after a full day on campus. I was exhausted."

She didn't care. And I didn't apologize.

Maybe that should have told me something right then and there.

Lessons in Love and a Luggage

Rachel was still upset about the party.

It had been weeks since I fell asleep in Mike's room while the party raged on outside, but she wouldn't let it go. On another date, she brought it up again, her frustration evident.

"It was uncool of you to come all the way to Philadelphia just to sleep," she said, crossing her arms.

I sighed. "I was tired."

"That's not the point."

"But it is the point. I drove three hours to see you. I wasn't planning to fall asleep—it just happened."

She shook her head, clearly unsatisfied. I was frustrated; she was frustrated. We kept going in circles, neither of us willing to budge.

Later, I talked to Andrea about it. She had a way of listening without judgment, of offering advice without making me feel small. After hearing me out, she smiled gently and said, "You should talk to someone older. A man who's been where you are."

That's how I found Arthur.

For the next few months, he became my mentor, the man who helped me navigate my relationships with women. I told him about Rachel and how upset she had been about me sleeping at her party.

"I don't get it," I admitted. "Why is she so mad about something so small?"

Arthur was quiet for a moment. Then he asked, "What did you go to the party for? To have fun, or to sleep?"

"To have fun, of course. But I had been driving for three hours. I was exhausted."

He nodded, as if he expected that answer. "Here's the thing— women process emotions as facts. If she feels like what you did was wrong, then to her, it was wrong. And what do you do when you hurt someone, even if you don't think you did anything wrong?"

I exhaled. "You apologize."

Arthur smiled. "Exactly."

That was a harsh reality to swallow. It wasn't about logic; it was about feelings. And if Rachel felt hurt, then it was my responsibility to acknowledge that, whether or not I agreed.

So, I admitted I was wrong and apologized to Rachel. It smoothed things over… for a while.

But I wasn't done making mistakes.

Three weeks later, it was Rachel's birthday.

I wanted to get her something special, something meaningful. So I went shopping, picked out what I thought was the perfect gift, had it wrapped, and took it to her birthday party.

I watched eagerly as she opened her presents, waiting for the moment she would get to mine. I had imagined the look on her face—the wide smile, the excitement, maybe even a delighted hug or a kiss on the cheek.

Then she unwrapped it.

She stared at it for a long moment before finally saying, "Thank you… it's very practical."

That was it.

No squeal of excitement. No glowing appreciation. Just practical.

I felt a lump form in my throat. I had expected her to love it because I loved it. But it was obvious—Rachel did not love it.

I should have known better.

So, once again, I turned to Arthur.

I recounted the whole story to him, right down to Rachel's lackluster reaction. He listened patiently, then leaned back with a knowing smile.

"What did you give her?" he asked.

"It was a good gift, man. I gave Rachel a luggage set."

Arthur blinked. "A luggage set? Like... suitcases?"

"Yes."

There was a moment of silence. Then Arthur burst out laughing. He laughed so hard he had to clutch his stomach.

For five straight minutes, he laughed.

Finally, wiping his eyes, he looked at me and said, "Son... you gave a woman luggage for her birthday?"

I nodded, confused. "Yeah. What's wrong with that?"

Arthur just shook his head. "Oh, man. You basically told her, 'Here, babe. Pack your bags.'"

I groaned. "It wasn't like that! It was a nice luggage set. I thought she'd love it."

Arthur chuckled. "Look, it's a great gift—for someone going on a trip, or maybe for Christmas. But for a birthday? Women don't want practical. They want thoughtful. Something that says, 'I see you. I understand you.'"

I let that sink in.

I had thought I was being thoughtful, but I had been thoughtful on my terms. I had chosen something I found useful, something I would have appreciated, without considering what she would have wanted.

It was another lesson, one of many Arthur would teach me.

And once again, I had to do something I was quickly getting used to.

I had to apologize.

The Wisdom of Arthur

I was beginning to understand why Rachel didn't like the luggage set.

It was dense of me to think women saw things the same way men did. Even Arthur, my mentor in all things love and relationships, could barely believe that was the gift I had chosen for her birthday.

"You're not supposed to give 'good' things to a woman on her birthday," he told me, shaking his head. "You give things that have emotional value, sentimental value, or financial value. Not practical things."

That was just one of many lessons Arthur taught me.

Having an older, wiser man in my life had become a necessity, not a luxury. Without Arthur's guidance, I would have continued stumbling through relationships, clueless about what truly mattered, unintentionally hurting the women I pursued. I needed his perspective. I needed his wisdom. And I needed his honesty—especially when it came to making the decision.

I had three women in my life—Rachel, Gabela, and Lauren.

It was time to choose.

Arthur, as always, approached the decision with calm precision. He didn't ask me who was the most beautiful. He didn't ask me who I had the most fun with. Instead, he asked me a simple but revealing question:

"What do you like about each of them?"

I thought for a moment and answered as honestly as I could.

"Gabela is very smart," I said. "I love the way she carries herself. She's adorable and attractive."

"Rachel is so cute. You could cuddle her all day. She's beautiful and always dresses well."

"Lauren is a fashionista. I love her sense of style and fashion."

Arthur didn't say much in response. Instead, he handed me a book.

Just Between Friends.

"Read this," he said. "Then we'll talk."

I didn't even have to finish the book to realize what Arthur was trying to teach me. When we met again, he simply looked at me and said, "You're more concerned with their appearance than with their hearts.

That hit hard.

I had been so caught up in what these women looked like, in how they carried themselves, in how they dressed, that I had barely considered their character. Their personalities. The things that would actually matter in a long-term relationship.

Arthur was right—I had been focused on the chase, not the end result.

He advised me to spend time truly observing these women. To pay attention to how they acted, not just with me, but with their friends, with strangers, with the people who couldn't do anything for them.

So I did.

And what I found was eye-opening.

When I spent time with Gabela and her friends, she later told me that some of them had asked her what she saw in me. They didn't understand why she liked me, why she was even considering me as a partner.

I never asked her what she said in response. Maybe I didn't want to know.

Lauren was another story. After a few dates, she admitted to me, "I'm not sure if I even like you."

Was that really her talking? Or was that the influence of her friends? Either way, it told me everything I needed to know.

The Decision

When I took a step back, when I really looked at things, the choice became clear.

It was Rachel.

Rachel and I just worked together. There was no second-guessing, no forced effort to make things fit. With her, I felt understood. At ease. At home.

It took me almost a year to decide, but when I finally did, I knew it was the right choice.

Arthur had guided me through the confusion, but the decision was mine.

One night, while at dinner with Rachel and her friends, she excused herself to go to the restroom.

The moment she stepped away from the table, I took a deep breath, dropped to one knee, and pulled out the ring.

When she returned, before she even had time to process what was happening, I asked,

"Rachel, would you like to be my fiancée?"

She gasped.

For a moment, she was too shocked to speak. Then, suddenly, she broke into a wide smile and shouted, "YES!"

The room erupted in cheers.

I was ecstatic. I couldn't believe I was finally engaged to Rachel.

Thanks to Arthur, I had made a decision I was sure of.

When I broke the news to Gabela and Lauren, they both acted like they were happy for me. And maybe, on some level, they were. But I later learned the truth.

Gabela was angry.

She never spoke to me again after that night.

Lauren, on the other hand, seemed too lost in the dating game to even care.

But that was okay. I had found my person.

Having a male mentor—someone who had lived through the struggles I was just beginning to understand—was a blessing I couldn't ignore.

Without Arthur, I don't know how many more women I would have chased after, how many more relationships I would have ruined simply because I had no idea what I was doing.

There would have been more heartbreak, more confusion, more frustration.

Maybe even enough to make me stop believing in love altogether. But Arthur had given me a gift greater than just advice—he had given me perspective.

And because of that, I was finally ready to love right.

7

I Don't Have to Wonder

My relationship with Rachel was unlike any I had before.

She was the first woman who made me want to settle down, to build a life with someone. With Rachel, I didn't have to second-guess my feelings, didn't have to wonder if I was making the right choice. It was clear, simple. She felt the same way—she couldn't wait to get married, and for the first time in my life, neither could I.

I had proposed to her at the end of the summer, and before the reality of wedding planning could fully sink in, she invited me to spend Thanksgiving with her family in Syracuse.

Rachel had been raised by a single mother, alongside a brother and a sister. Family was important to her, and now that we were engaged, it was important to me too. This wasn't just about us anymore—it was about becoming part of each other's world.

The night before Thanksgiving, I drove from New York to Philadelphia to pick her up, and together, we made the long trek to Syracuse.

It was a journey that tested my patience, my stamina, and my ability to stay awake on the road. The traffic was brutal, the snow relentless, and the roads treacherous with slush. But somehow, despite it all, it felt... good. The slow pace gave us time to talk, to reflect, to share stories we hadn't yet told each other.

Somewhere between New York and Syracuse, between stretches of icy highway and moments of exhausted laughter, I realized how much I loved her.

The conversation in the car was comforting, reassuring.

I felt content.

But the fun of the road trip eventually wore off. Fatigue crept in, making my eyes heavy, my body sluggish. We needed a break.

That's how we ended up at a dimly lit roadside inn, a few meters off the highway. It wasn't much—just a worn-out diner attached to a motel, the kind of place that looked like it had seen better days.

The coffee was terrible.

But what kept us there wasn't the coffee—it was the way we made a game out of it.

We joked about the place, about how it looked like the setting of some low-budget horror movie, and how Jason from Friday the 13th was probably lurking in the back, waiting for his next victims. The more we talked, the more ridiculous the stories became. Laughter kept us warm.

That was the thing about Rachel.

Even in the middle of exhaustion, in a bleak little inn with bad coffee and flickering lights, she made me feel like we were exactly where we were supposed to be.

After a couple of hours, the snow finally let up, and we got back on the road.

By the time we reached her mother's house, I was drained, my body begging for rest. But as I pulled into the driveway, as I saw the glow of warm lights in the windows, I knew—this was the beginning of something real.

Rachel was my future.

And for the first time, I didn't have to wonder.

A Thanksgiving to Remember

Thanksgiving with Rachel's family was better than I could have ever hoped for.

From the moment I stepped inside her mother's home, I felt something I hadn't expected—a sense of belonging.

It wasn't just the warmth of the house, the rich smell of turkey and cinnamon filling the air, or the festive decorations that seemed to glow in the dim light. It was the way everyone welcomed me, how they made space for me at their table, how, for the first time in my life, I felt like I was exactly where I was supposed to be.

Rachel's mother was beautiful, graceful in a way that made me think of Rachel in the years to come. If genetics had anything to do with it, I had no doubt Rachel would age just as well.

The evening was lively. Laughter filled the room as family and friends gathered around the long dining table, passing dishes, sharing stories. There was one guest in particular who stood out—a middle-aged man, a pastor from Rachel's mother's church. He wasn't just a family friend; he had a crush on Rachel's mother, and he wasn't subtle about it.

It was entertaining watching him try to work his charm.

The man could talk—a parrot in human form, filling every silent space with words. If there was a lull in conversation, he took it upon himself to fill it. He told stories, quoted scriptures, asked and answered his own questions, all while occasionally sneaking hopeful glances at Rachel's mother.

If he was hoping to win her over, I had my doubts. Women, in my experience, didn't care much for talkative men.

Still, I had never experienced a holiday quite like this before—a house full of people who genuinely enjoyed each other's company, where laughter was easy and love was evident in the smallest gestures.

But as quickly as the warmth of the night settled over me, it was shattered in an instant.

A sudden crash echoed from the kitchen—the sound of a plate hitting the floor—followed immediately by raised voices.

I moved quickly, following the commotion.

There, in the kitchen, I found Rachel and her sister locked in a heated argument, their voices bouncing off the walls, turning the heart of the home into a battleground.

Rachel was furious, her words sharp with accusation. She was scolding her sister for neglecting their mother, for not giving her the attention and care she deserved at her age.

Her sister didn't back down.

The tension in the room was thick, heavy, suffocating.

I stepped forward, instinct taking over. "Hey," I said, my voice calm but firm. "It's Thanksgiving. Let's cool off, alright? For tonight, let's just enjoy being here, together."

The words hung in the air.

For a moment, neither of them spoke.

I wasn't sure if my attempt at peace had worked or if I had just inserted myself into something deeper than I could understand.

But what I did know was this—beneath all the joy, the laughter, the warmth of this home, there were fractures. Old wounds. Unspoken tensions simmering just beneath the surface.

And as much as I wanted to be a part of Rachel's world, I was beginning to realize that love wasn't just about fitting in.

It was about understanding the complexities that came with it.

Seeing Rachel Clearly

I hadn't expected Rachel to turn on me so suddenly.

When I stepped in to calm the argument between her and her sister, I thought my presence would be enough to diffuse the situation—that the reminder of a guest in the house might pull them back from the edge of their anger.

I was wrong.

Rachel spun on me, her voice sharp, her eyes flashing with fury.

"You're taking her side?" she snapped.

I was stunned.

"No, I just think—"

"She's always disrespecting me and Mom, and now you're standing here defending her?"

Nothing I said could calm her down.

Rachel ignored me for the rest of the night, her frustration simmering beneath the surface. The warmth of the evening was gone. She wouldn't even look at me during dinner, and when it ended, her sister was the one who showed me to my room.

As I lay in bed that night, staring at the ceiling, I replayed everything over and over in my mind.

Was I wrong to step in? Should I have just let them fight? Was this just the stress of the holidays, or was it something more?

I had brought a gift for Rachel, a small gesture of love I had planned to give her after dinner. But instead, I left it on the table for her to find.

I didn't see her again that night.

The next morning, when she finally saw the gift, she apologized. She said she regretted how the night had gone, how she had treated me. She seemed sincere, but something about it still unsettled me.

And then I remembered something my father once told me during one of our father-son talks:

"If a woman disrespects her family and mother right in front of you, then you can't expect her to do better for you and your family."

That thought clung to me like a shadow.

Back in New York, I sought out Arthur, hoping for clarity, for guidance.

"You must know your fiancée in all aspects if you want to marry her," he told me. "And to do that, you need to remove the distance from your equation. Give your relationship a chance to flourish or fail—but let it do so honestly."

I knew what I had to do next.

I asked Rachel if she would move to New Jersey to be closer to me.

It wasn't a proposal made lightly. I wanted to see her—not just during dates, not just in planned, polished moments, but in everyday life. I needed to understand who she was outside of the romance, outside of the excitement of engagement.

After some thought, she agreed.

I reached out to Mandy, a woman I had met at church. She was in her fifties, kind, and had a spare bedroom in her apartment in East Orange. She agreed to let Rachel stay with her. On the surface, their relationship seemed like a mentor-mentee dynamic, and it felt like a stable solution.

Once Rachel settled in, I moved closer too.

We fell into an easy routine—morning coffee runs together, then she would take my car while I was at work to run her errands.

Our proximity made things spontaneous, effortless. We didn't have to schedule dates; we simply lived them.

For a while, it felt good.

But then I decided to check in with Mandy.

The Truth Comes Out

Mandy had been meaning to talk to me. I could sense it in the way she smiled when we met for coffee, the way she measured her words carefully.

After some small talk, she finally asked, "How is it going with Rachel?"

I told her it was good, though she was still struggling to find a job.

Mandy nodded, then leaned in slightly. "I need to be honest with you."

I braced myself.

"Rachel isn't looking for a job," she said bluntly. "She sits at home all day making calls and doing nothing."

Her words hit me like a punch to the gut.

That wasn't the Rachel I thought I knew.

I had assumed she was trying, that she was just facing challenges in the job market. I had even been considering setting up a bank account for her and transferring some money to help her with expenses.

Mandy's next words stopped me cold.

"Don't do that," she warned. "It will set the wrong expectations for your relationship. Your partner needs to be able to provide for herself, so that one day, she can support you when you need it."

And just like that, my father's words echoed in my mind again.

Was I about to make a mistake? Was I ignoring warning signs I should have been paying attention to?

Rachel was beautiful, charming, fun to be with. But now, I had seen flashes of something deeper—anger, entitlement, a willingness to let others take care of things for her.

For the first time, I wondered:

Was Rachel really the woman I should marry? Or was I just blinded by the idea of love?

A Moment of Doubt

The night I proposed to Rachel, I called my parents in Ghana, eager to share my excitement.

My mother, ever the nurturer, asked me one simple question: "Is this what you want?"

"Yes," I told her. And with that, she offered her congratulations.

When my father got on the phone, I expected him to ask me the same thing. Or maybe ask if I loved her. Instead, his first question caught me off guard.

"Does she work with her hands?"

I paused, not knowing how to answer. It was an odd thing to ask. My mind raced—was he asking if she had a job? If she was industrious? If she could cook?

Before I could respond, he continued.

"Your wife should be able to assist you during tough times."

There was a certainty in his voice, the weight of experience behind his words. My father and mother had been married for over fifty years, standing side by side through every storm. He wasn't just asking about Rachel's career. He was asking if she had the substance—the resilience—to hold a marriage together when life got hard.

"My mother was able to shoulder the responsibility when I couldn't work because of my stroke," he explained.

His words clung to me like a shadow.

Later, when Mandy told me that Rachel wasn't even looking for a job, I felt my father's wisdom echoing in my mind. Was I about to make a mistake?

The Coffee That Changed Everything

That Saturday morning, Rachel and I took our usual walk to the coffee house. It was supposed to be a simple, comforting ritual. But something felt off.

I held her hand, trying to picture our future. What would our life be like together? What memories would we fall back on when times got tough? What dreams did we share?

I came up empty.

We had no memories to hold onto. No dreams we had built together.

The realization hit me as we sat down with our coffee, the silence between us louder than anything. The small, lonely corner we had chosen only amplified what I was feeling inside.

Had I made a mistake?

Had I gotten engaged to the wrong woman?

How I Got Here

To understand why I was suddenly struggling, I had to retrace my steps—how I got into this situation in the first place.

At one point, I had three solid, meaningful relationships.

Three women who, at different moments, I had seen as potential life partners.

A week before I proposed to Rachel, I had taken Lauren to my company's holiday party. I introduced her to my coworkers, and she charmed everyone in the room.

One woman, an older executive secretary, pulled me aside afterward.

"I know women," she told me. "And this girl complements you. You should marry her."

That night, I wrestled with my decision. I liked Lauren. She was fun, stylish, and easy to talk to. But there was one problem—I couldn't handle her emotions. She cried over everything, even things I thought were trivial.

Could I live with that?

The answer was no.

Then there was Gabela. Confident. Mature. But also a bit controlling.

The moment I knew she wasn't the one?

She called me out of the blue and said, "I heard through the grapevine that you might propose to me. You do know that's a decision we need to make together, right?"

She wasn't asking me—she was telling me.

That was all I needed to hear. Still, I spoke to a married friend for advice.

He told me to ask myself one fundamental question:

"Can you live with her exactly as she is for the rest of your life?"

I didn't even hesitate.

No.

And so, by process of elimination, I had chosen Rachel.

She didn't cry over small things. She wasn't controlling. She was beautiful, fun, and easy to be around.

At the time, it felt like the right choice.

But now, sitting in that coffee shop, staring at her across the table, I felt a sinking feeling in my gut.

I had been so focused on what I didn't want that I never truly considered what I did want.

And now, I wasn't sure if I had chosen wisely.

The Truth Behind the Proposal

The full story of why I proposed to Rachel wasn't as romantic as I wished it had been.

That week, when I traveled to Philadelphia to see her, I had already ordered the diamond engagement ring. But deep down, I knew I wasn't ready. I sensed Rachel's impatience—there was an unspoken urgency in her, a silent pressure that made me afraid.

I feared that if I didn't propose soon, I would lose her completely.

And so, that afternoon, I gathered some of her friends for lunch at a seafood restaurant. The moment felt orchestrated, rehearsed. Sometime during the meal, I got down on one knee and asked her to be my fiancée.

She said yes.

The weight of uncertainty was momentarily lifted. I felt relief. Maybe even joy.

But as I drove back to New York that night, alone with my thoughts, doubt crept in.

Had I made the right decision?

I told myself the doubt would pass. And for a time, it did. The moment I put the ring on her finger, I was sure.

But when I asked her to move to New Jersey, the doubt returned.

That summer, life presented me with a new opportunity.

I was promoted at work and offered a management role in Texas. It was a career-defining moment, the kind of opportunity that would set the trajectory of my professional life.

I was excited when I shared the news with Rachel.

She wasn't.

She was against the move. She said it would take her too far from her family. She didn't want to start over, didn't want to build a new life in a city where she had no connections.

I didn't fight her on it.

After all, this was the woman I had just asked to move to New Jersey for me. How could I now ask her to pack up and move again?

So, I passed on the opportunity.

At the time, I convinced myself it was a small sacrifice.

But in the days and weeks that followed, I felt something shift between us.

A distance I couldn't quite name.

Rachel still hadn't found a job. Mandy's concerns about her lack of effort weighed on me. And more than that, I began noticing other cracks in our relationship—small, insignificant things that, when put together, painted a much bigger picture.

SO GOOD TO LOVE A WOMAN

If there was one thing Rachel and I truly shared, it was our love for music.

We had a tradition: after every wedding we attended, we would return to my apartment, make dinner together, and then spend the night listening to music, letting jazz fill the silence between us.

Those nights made me feel close to her, reminded me of why I had proposed in the first place.

But one night, it all unraveled.

We had just finished dinner, the evening unfolding as it always did. Then, as we were about to settle in, she asked if she could borrow my entire collection of new jazz CDs.

I hesitated.

I told her no.

Not because I didn't love her. Not because I wanted to upset her.

But because I didn't trust that she would take care of them.

And for the first time, I realized—if I didn't trust her with something as small as my music, how could I trust her with my life?

The argument that followed wasn't loud or dramatic, but it revealed something I hadn't been willing to see before: something was missing in our relationship.

I didn't know what, exactly.

But I knew we needed to talk, to figure out what had evaporated between us before it was too late.

The Question I Couldn't Answer

And so, that morning at the coffee house, as I sat across from Rachel, trying to piece together what had gone wrong, she did something that caught me off guard.

She reached across the table, took my left hand in hers, and ran her fingers over the ring she wore.

Then she looked into my eyes and asked, "What do you like about the ring you gave me?"

I drew a blank.

I opened my mouth, but no words came.

I had no poetic answer, no romantic sentiment to offer her.

Before I could stumble through an excuse, she smiled—a small, knowing smile—and said, "I guess words can't describe your thoughts."

And in that moment, something inside me cracked.

I felt sad. Not because I had failed to answer her question.

But because I had nothing to give to the woman I had engaged.

And worse—because somehow, I was still hoping to find something that wasn't there.

A Moment of Clarity

My fears were confirmed when we began marriage counseling.

Up until that point, I had tried to push my doubts aside, reasoning that no relationship was perfect, that love required patience and understanding. But during one particular session, those doubts—the ones I had tried so hard to ignore—became impossible to overlook.

The couple leading our counseling session asked me a seemingly simple question:

"Can you see yourself moving outside the U.S. to live back where you were born?"

I nodded. I had always considered the possibility. Life had a way of shifting plans, and I wanted to keep my options open.

Then they turned to Rachel.

"If the situation ever arose where he had to move outside the U.S. for work or any other reason, would you go with him?"

Her answer came quickly.

"No, because he would have to change jobs if that ever came up."

And as if that wasn't enough, she went on to suggest an alternative.

"We could always move to Syracuse, where my family lives."

I felt something inside me snap.

It was subtle—an internal shift, a moment of realization so sharp it cut through every rationalization I had made for her.

I excused myself and asked to use the bathroom.

The pastor directed me to the one in the basement, and as I walked back from the restroom, I found someone waiting for me.

The pastor's wife.

She didn't mince words.

"I don't think Rachel is the woman for you."

I stood frozen, shocked by her bluntness.

She wasn't guessing. She wasn't offering a vague warning. She was telling me, point-blank, that she saw something in my relationship that deeply concerned her.

I had to know more.

"What do you mean?" I asked, my voice cautious.

She sighed. "My husband and I have counseled many couples, and we don't feel good about this arrangement. The fights you have, the way you two argue—even in front of us—it's concerning. And that incident at Thanksgiving? That wasn't a fluke. That was who she is."

Her words were hitting me like waves, each one making me stumble a little more.

"She doesn't compromise," the pastor's wife continued. "She already made you pass up a great career opportunity, and now she's asking you to move to her hometown. She's thinking about herself, not about both of you. This is not a partnership. It's a one-sided decision-making process where you're expected to adjust, but she won't."

I felt my heart pounding.

I had been so focused on trying to make things work, on convincing myself that every relationship had challenges, that I hadn't stopped to ask the real question:

Was Rachel actually willing to build a life with me, or was she only focused on the life she wanted for herself?

A New Perspective

I had always believed in the wisdom of older men. Arthur had shaped so much of my understanding about relationships. But in that moment, I realized the equal importance of older women.

Here was a woman, someone with years of experience, someone who had seen countless relationships rise and fall, telling me what I had refused to see for myself.

And she was right.

Rachel wasn't supportive. She wasn't willing to compromise.

She was standing in the way of my dreams, my goals, and the life we were supposed to build together.

I had been blind to it for so long, but now?

Now, I saw it with terrifying clarity.

I walked back into the counseling session, my mind still reeling. The pastor looked at me expectantly.

"Have you come to a decision?" he asked.

I took a deep breath, looked at Rachel, and then said the words that had been forming in my heart for weeks:

"This isn't going to work."

For the first time in a long time, I wasn't thinking about what Rachel wanted.

I was thinking about me.

Because love isn't about one person dictating the terms. It isn't about making endless sacrifices without receiving the same in return.

It's about two people—together, equally committed, equally willing to compromise, equally invested in building something that lasts.

Rachel wasn't willing.

And now, finally, I wasn't willing either.

The Breaking Point

If there was one piece of advice my father had given me that I never forgot, it was this:

"Make sure you marry someone who likes to work—someone who can support and complement what you do."

He had seen enough life to know that love alone wasn't enough. Life had its struggles, and a true partner was someone who could stand beside you, contribute, and carry the weight when needed.

As we went through more marriage counseling sessions, that advice echoed in my mind.

Rachel still had not found a job.

The issue kept coming up—her position on work itself, not just job hunting, but whether she truly wanted to work. Each time, she had excuses. The economy was tough. She was still figuring things out. She wasn't sure what she wanted to do.

At first, I tried to be patient. But as the weeks passed, I started considering something drastic—postponing the wedding until she found a job.

But that didn't seem to shake her urgency to find work.

She wasn't enthused about working. She wasn't trying.

And that was it.

Eight days before the wedding, I called it off.

The End

She cried.

I cried.

But deep down, we both knew it was for the best.

We met one last time at our usual coffee shop, where we had spent so many hours talking about our relationship, our plans, our future. But that day, for the first time, we spoke with complete honesty.

We admitted to each other what we had avoided for so long—we didn't love each other enough to make sacrifices for one another, let alone get married.

She took off the engagement ring and placed it in my hand.

We said our goodbyes.

And as I walked out, I felt something I hadn't expected—relief.

The weight on my shoulders was gone.

The expectations, the compromises I was always making, the doubts I had ignored—all of it had lifted.

I walked down the street, staring at the diamond ring in my palm, wondering what to do with it.

A Little Girl and a Prayer

In hindsight, I should have left it with Rachel. Maybe she would have thrown it away. Maybe she would have kept it as a reminder of what almost was.

But instead, something unexpected happened.

I heard a giggle.

I looked up and saw a little girl, maybe eight years old, playing at the corner of the street with her nanny.

Something in me—some quiet impulse I didn't fully understand—made me walk up to her.

I placed the ring in her tiny hand and said, "I pray you find true love. Remember—never settle for less."

The girl and her nanny looked at me like I was crazy.

I just smiled and walked away.

To this day, I wonder about that little girl.

I hope she found her true love.

Signs I Should Have Seen

Looking back, the signs had always been there.

Rachel loved talking to others about me, but never about our relationship. It was never about us, about how she felt for me, about what we dreamed of together.

Instead, it was always about what I did. What I had accomplished.

She liked bragging about me.

She liked being associated with my success.

That wasn't love. That was status.

And then there was the comment she made early in our relationship—the one that should have given me pause.

She had once told me that a close friend of hers had asked, "Why are you with him? Why not one of the American guys we know?"

It reminded me of what Gabela had told me as well—that some of her friends didn't understand what she saw in me.

I had shrugged it off at the time, but I shouldn't have.

Was Rachel uncomfortable dating an African? Would she have preferred someone else? Or was it just that, deep down, she didn't see a future with me the way I had wanted to believe she did?

We never talked about it.

But we should have.

Not long after Rachel and I broke up, I had a second chance at work.

A new promotion came up—this time, I took it.

I packed my bags and moved to Baytown, Texas, as a senior engineer at a refinery.

If you've ever heard of Baytown, you know—it's not exactly a city of romance. It's a place where a single man can take a step back and reset his priorities.

For the next two years, nothing romantic happened in my life.

No dating. No engagement rings. No more near-mistakes.

I needed time.

I didn't know what I was searching for, only that I wasn't ready to search at all.

So I threw myself into other things.

Basketball games. Texas rodeos. Anything to keep my mind occupied.

I wasn't sure when I'd be ready to love again.

But one thing I was sure of?

The next time I put a ring on a woman's finger, it would be because there was no doubt in my heart.

Blunder That Taught Me a Lesson

After my time in Texas, my company offered me another opportunity—a move to Louisiana for two more years. But before I could make that decision, I knew I needed a break. I had to travel to Ghana to see my father.

It had been three years since my breakup with Rachel, and during that time, I had become withdrawn. My father's health had been declining since his stroke, and I needed to spend time with him. But while I was there, something else became painfully clear.

People around me noticed my emotional distance, particularly when it came to women. It was as though I had shut that part of myself off. A good friend, trying to break me out of my shell, introduced me to a colleague of his who worked at an insurance company.

He encouraged me to ask her out.

So, I did. I called her, asked her on a date, and she accepted.

It was Christmas Eve, December 24th. We went out for dinner. The evening was fine, pleasant even—nothing remarkable, just a nice meal and casual conversation. We finished dinner by 8:00

p.m. I dropped her off at her place, thanked her for the evening, and thought everything had gone smoothly.

But when I got home, my brother was waiting for me. His expression was a mixture of concern and amusement.

His first words were, "What in God's name is wrong with you? Why would you treat the lady that way?"

I was taken aback. I couldn't fathom what had gone wrong. I told him that our dinner had gone fine, only for him to tell me that the girl had called his colleague—furious. She was upset because she had expected more from the night.

She had expected the night to go longer, especially considering it was Christmas Eve. She was disappointed that I had ended the date at 9:00 p.m. when most people her age were out partying and celebrating the holiday.

That's when I realized my mistake.

It had been stupid to take her out on Christmas Eve, then send her home so early.

I was clearly out of practice, and my game had lost its sharpness.

My brother and father found the whole situation hilarious. They both laughed it off and encouraged me to do better.

Apology and the Lesson

I didn't waste time feeling embarrassed for long. I went back to her place to apologize for my mistake. I was nervous—very nervous—but to my relief, she accepted my apology graciously.

We ended up spending the rest of the evening together, but this time, we stayed in. We had a great time just talking, enjoying each other's company.

Over time, we became good friends. And though we never dated seriously, that night and my blunder taught me a valuable lesson—about being more considerate, about understanding expectations, and about how important it is to genuinely connect with someone rather than just going through the motions.

It was a humbling experience, but one that helped me realize that I still had a lot to learn—especially when it came to relationships. It was a rude awakening, but a necessary one.

After two quiet years in Houston, I was ready for a change. My next move took me to Baton Rouge, Louisiana—close enough to New Orleans to fuel my love for jazz, yet far enough to give me the fresh start I needed.

Baton Rouge turned out to be exactly what I was looking for.

I settled in, found a local church, and became part of its singles ministry. Soon, I had a circle of friends, and my days were filled with laughter, music, and a sense of ease I hadn't felt in years. Life was simple, and for the first time in a long time, I was happy.

But more than anything, I realized something profound—I had changed.

Gone was the man who rushed into relationships with a mix of excitement and blind faith. Gone was the man who ignored red flags and made compromises for the sake of keeping things together.

Rachel had been a hard lesson, but one that left a lasting impact.

I didn't want to repeat the same mistakes.

So I was cautious. Not guarded, but intentional. I paid attention—to conversations, to dynamics, to how I felt around people. I focused on building friendships rather than diving straight into romantic relationships.

I no longer viewed dating as a means to an end, as something that had to follow a structured timeline toward marriage.

Instead, I let things unfold naturally.

For the first time, I truly understood that a relationship wasn't just about romance—it was about knowing the person, about trusting the person, about finding someone whose life could intertwine with mine in a way that felt effortless.

And so, in Baton Rouge, surrounded by music, friendship, and a newfound clarity, I embraced this new approach to love.

Not as a race.

Not as a checklist.

But as a journey.

8

She's Gonna Make It

Coming out of my dating slump was a slow process, but it was exactly what I needed.

Introductions were made.

Weekend dates happened.

Church activities filled my time.

And somewhere between all of it, I found myself again.

Unlike before, I wasn't rushing into anything. I wasn't looking for someone to marry. I was looking to understand—to build real friendships and learn more about the women I was meeting. And in the process, I learned a lot about myself.

Rachel had once made me a jazz recording—a full hour of music interspersed with her voice, telling me how much she appreciated me. I had listened to that tape for months after our breakup. It had helped me heal, to hear her speak about the qualities she admired in me. But in the end, that recording had also revealed something else: the gulf between us.

A gulf that neither of us had been willing to risk bridging.

But now, I was in a new place, emotionally and physically. And as I dated, two women stood out to me in ways that changed me forever.

A Fragile Friendship

Daniella was a slender, elegant brunette. She had a quiet grace about her, but underneath that, I could sense her fragility.

We went on several dates, and as time passed, we developed a deep friendship. I often picked her up from work, and we would spend hours talking. She was more open with me than any woman I had ever known, sharing the most intimate details of her struggles—her past with drugs, her history with abusive relationships.

While I admired her openness, it also scared me.

Could I take on that kind of emotional weight? Could I be what she needed?

Many nights, I sat with her through tears as she processed her past. And though I cared for her deeply, I held back. Something in me knew that this wasn't the right fit.

Then, one day, one of her friends approached me and said, "Daniella really likes you. She wants to know how you feel."

I had no good answer. I wasn't ready to commit.

When my response got back to Daniella, her reaction was clear—anger.

That was all the confirmation I needed.

I had to walk away.

Athena: The Woman Who Knew Me

Then there was Athena.

From the moment I met her, she lived up to the Greek goddess she was named after.

She was strong, confident, and stunningly beautiful. She carried herself with an effortless charm—a tomboyish energy mixed with undeniable femininity. She knew she was a woman, and she loved being one.

Unlike Daniella, Athena didn't just want to know about me. She wanted to understand me.

She was playful yet wise, strong yet soft, direct yet deeply caring.

Each time we were together, she felt like the perfect fit.

We could finish each other's sentences.

We challenged each other but never in a way that felt combative.

She knew how to read me—how to pull me out of my own head when I retreated, how to get me to open up even when I didn't want to. And yet, she deferred to me as if I was her everything.

We weren't just friends.

We weren't just dating.

We were something more.

And neither of us had the courage to say it out loud.

She would surprise me by cooking for me. Sometimes, she'd just show up at my place and tidy up, not because I asked, but because she wanted to. It was a small gesture, but it said everything—this was a woman raised in a strong household, raised to know how to care for a man while still knowing her own worth.

She was everything I had ever needed in a woman.

For a while, we felt like a married couple.

A Moment to Remember

In the summer of 1996, I bought a new Toyota Land Cruiser.

There was no one in the world I wanted to show it to more than her.

I was supposed to pick her up after her classes at LSU, so I drove straight from the dealership to campus.

There she was, standing in front of the student center, watching as I pulled up in this massive new truck.

She must have been wondering, Who on earth is driving this thing toward me?

I stopped right next to her, jumped out of the car, and the moment she realized it was me, her face lit up.

I will never forget the hug she gave me.

In that instant, she painted a memory I would carry for life.

She made me realize just how much I needed a woman in my life—not just any woman, but the right woman.

We both knew we had fallen in love.

But we never said it.

Maybe we were afraid of ruining what we had.

Maybe we didn't know how to navigate the shift from deep friendship to something more.

Or maybe… it was because no one around us expected it.

It became a secret we kept—even from ourselves.

A Goodbye That Broke Me

All too soon, my two-year work assignment came to an end.

She asked me, "Are you going back to New York?"

I nodded. "Yes. I have to."

That night, I quietly cried.

I didn't want to go back to New York without her.

But I also knew—I had to make sure I wasn't repeating the mistake I made with Rachel.

Love wasn't just about feelings.

It was about timing. About commitment. About knowing beyond a doubt that you were ready to take that step.

And at that moment, I didn't know.

So I left Baton Rouge.

I left Athena.

And I left a piece of my heart behind.

Daniella and Athena taught me something I had never fully grasped in my past relationships—I needed to keep my wits about me while dating.

Up until then, I had been swept up in emotions, in attraction, in the thrill of finding a connection. But now, I realized something even more important: I needed to figure out what I could and could not tolerate in a relationship.

I needed to define my non-negotiables.

What was out of my comfort zone? What would I never compromise on?

My time with Daniella showed me that emotional fragility, while endearing in some ways, could also be a burden I wasn't ready to carry. I admired her vulnerability, but I wasn't equipped to be the man she needed.

Athena, on the other hand, showed me what was possible—a relationship built on mutual respect, understanding, and effortless compatibility. She was the first woman who made me feel completely seen.

But timing is a cruel master, and love without timing is often just a beautiful tragedy.

The Shadow of Rachel

Even as I was moving forward, a part of me still looked back.

My relationship with Rachel had taught me hard lessons, but it also left behind what-ifs.

Looking back, I see now that I was much more in love with Rachel than she was with me.

She was apprehensive about marrying me. Her sorority sisters had made her question whether she should settle down with an African man. And I kept telling myself that if she truly loved me, she would have ignored them.

But she didn't.

She was looking for familiarity. For convenience.

Marriage to her wasn't about love—it was about checking off the right boxes. And even though I checked most of them, I was still an option, not the choice.

I was replaceable.

I was temporary.

One That Got Away

If men and women are truly honest with themselves, we all have that one person.

The person we wonder about.

The person who lingers in the back of our minds when we think about what could have been.

The one who makes us question whether we made the right decision.

For me, that person was Irene.

Yes, that Irene.

The same Irene I met when Professor Gabela was giving me a hard time.

She was breathtakingly beautiful. But more than that, she reminded me of something pure—of childhood memories, of innocent moments, of the kind of effortless companionship that doesn't need to be forced.

When I first met her, she was an undergrad at Barnard College while I was at Columbia.

I admired her. Not just for her beauty, but for her mind.

She was bold, intelligent, and never afraid to tell me exactly what she thought.

One afternoon, she sat with me and shared her plans to go to medical school. We talked for hours.

But never once did it occur to me that I might like her.

I just loved being in her presence.

She was so stunning to look at that when she dozed off on my couch during one of her visits, I found myself just staring—not in lust, not even in longing, but in pure admiration.

She left for medical school just before I graduated.

And then, five years passed.

And I saw her again.

The Night I Fell for Irene

It was the summer after I completed my company rotation in Baton Rouge. Life had settled into a rhythm, and I had been invited to a reunion party at the New York City Marriott Marquis.

Out of the blue, I called Irene.

I hadn't spoken to her in a long time, but something inside me needed to hear her voice. She was now doing her medical internship at Johns Hopkins University, deep in the throes of her journey to becoming a doctor.

We talked for hours.

There was something about talking to Irene that made time irrelevant. Our conversations always felt easy, unforced.

And then, on a whim, I asked her to come with me to the dance.

I half-expected her to decline—her life was busy, structured, demanding. But to my surprise, she agreed.

That afternoon, she flew in.

And oh, boy… she was breathtaking.

She wore a midnight blue evening dress that hugged her figure in all the right places, with a light blue shawl draped over her shoulders, softening her elegance with an air of effortless grace.

I couldn't even recall what I wore that night. It didn't matter.

All I knew was that I felt proud—proud to be in her presence, proud that this was the woman walking into that ballroom with me.

I picked her up from where she was staying in New Jersey, and what followed was the most enjoyable drive of my life.

The night was calm, draped in a soft drizzle that shimmered under the city lights. It felt as if the gods themselves were sprinkling silver jewels along our path, lighting up the streets just for us.

She reached over and took my hand as I drove.

Her hands were warm, soft, comforting.

For the first time in years—maybe even since my childhood—I felt the warmth of a woman in a way that wasn't just physical. It was something deeper, something unexplainable.

I had been around beautiful women before. I had dated, had relationships, even fallen in love.

But this?

This was different.

We arrived at the party, but the details of the event itself faded into the background.

I don't even remember if we danced.

What I do remember is talking—talking about life, about our past, about the people we had become in the years since we had last seen each other.

It was effortless, like slipping into a familiar song, one where you already know the lyrics without needing to think.

As the night stretched on, we left the main event and went to an after-party in New Jersey, conveniently close to my hotel. By the time we left, it was 2:00 a.m.

Rather than hail a cab, we decided to walk.

She took off her shoes, handed them to me, and wrapped her arm around my waist as we strolled down the quiet streets.

I would pay anything to relive that moment, even if just for a second.

When we arrived at my hotel, I opened the door for her. She walked in first, then suddenly turned and pulled me toward her, spinning me in front of the mirror.

I hugged her, and as I looked past her into our reflection, I was bowled over.

What a sight.

What a woman.

Her beauty was undeniable, but it wasn't just that. It was the way she carried herself, the way she fit into my space as if she had always belonged there.

There, in that moment, I knew—God had created this one with joy.

Women are designed to be pleasing to the eye, to evoke emotion, to stir something deep inside a man. But Irene was more than that. She was a mystery, a woman whose very presence made me question how I had lived so long without her.

That night, she could have been anywhere. She could have been with anyone.

But she was with me.

And that's a mystery men may never fully understand—why does a woman choose the man she chooses?

Is it logic? Is it fate? Is it an unspoken energy that binds two souls together?

That night, it reminded me of the way a horse bonds with its owner.

A horse is strong, wild, untamed in its natural form. But when it trusts, when it chooses loyalty, it becomes the most devoted, controlled, and obedient creature on earth.

A woman's love is the same.

When a woman truly bonds with a man, her loyalty is unyielding.

And that night, Irene had chosen to be with me.

We talked until we both fell asleep.

And when I woke up, I found her sleeping soundly on top of me, like a child resting in the safest place she could find.

That was the moment I knew—this woman was special.

She was different.

And I had fallen for her.

In the weeks and months that followed, I visited her in Baltimore.

She visited me in Boston.

We built something beautiful, something neither of us had planned for but both of us knew was real.

I had finally found the kind of love that wasn't forced, that wasn't built on expectations, that wasn't just about checking the right boxes.

I had found her.

The Night I Lost Irene

One weekend, I decided to fly to Baltimore for a date with her.

She had a late shift at work, so we planned it carefully—I would take a late flight, and she would pick me up from the airport. From there, we would head straight to a local jazz club for dinner.

It wasn't our first date, but in a way, it felt like it.

You see, every time I had visited her before, I had taken a cab from the airport to her place. This was the first time she was picking me up herself. It felt... special.

As I strolled through the arrival hall, I saw her coming up the escalator.

She wore a pair of beautiful brown wool pants, a white sweater, and an off-white silk undershirt that made her glow under the dim airport lights.

She looked gorgeous.

We hugged, and she took my hand.

But as I looked into her eyes, something was missing.

I searched them for the warmth, the excitement, the unspoken energy that had always been there before.

Instead, I saw something else.

Her eyes were glassy, teary—not from happiness, but from something burdensome. Something heavy.

"Is something wrong?" I asked gently.

She hesitated, then forced a small smile. "No, nothing's wrong."

But I knew better.

That night, as we sat together, she finally told me.

She had been assaulted by a man she had trusted.

And in that moment, I understood everything—the hesitation, the guardedness, the quiet distance I had felt growing between us.

She was struggling to be vulnerable with me.

She wanted to let me in.

But she was scared.

All I could do was hold her.

I wished I could take away her pain. I wished I could erase what had happened, replace the hurt with warmth, with laughter, with all the things I wanted to give her.

But some wounds run too deep.

And that night, I realized something else—I couldn't let her get away.

She was too special. Too rare.

Irene was the kind of woman a man finds once in a lifetime.

Wrong Place, The Wrong Time

Irene fit into my life like a missing puzzle piece.

She was the girl who reminded me of childhood memories—the laughter, the innocence, the effortless companionship that made love feel natural.

But I met her at the wrong time.

I was in business school in Boston, surrounded by a culture that didn't nurture love—it devoured it.

Business school was like a meat-packing district.

Men and women took a break from adulthood, looking for hookups instead of commitment.

Couples who arrived together? They left graduated and divorced.

Couples who met in business school? Their relationships were fleeting affairs, built on nothing but attraction and convenience, leaving behind nothing but hurt.

It was the worst place to fall in love.

And I was in the worst state of mind to handle it.

I was still wrestling with ghosts from my past. I carried the weight of past relationships—the doubts, the mistakes, the what-ifs that haunted me.

Irene visited me in Boston several times, but her hesitation lingered. And her hesitation made me question my readiness.

Was I really ready for her? Or was I just holding on because I was afraid of losing something I knew was rare?

Instead of facing that question, I did what so many men do when they're lost. I withdrew. I spent more time with my guy friends—men who had been through bad relationships, men who resented women.

Every weekend became a chorus of complaints, of bitterness, of stories about how women had hurt them, how love was a fool's game. I let those voices drown out the truth in my heart. And before I even realized it, I lost Irene.

Regret in Hindsight

Looking back, I know the truth.

Irene didn't leave because she didn't care.

She left because she needed certainty.

She needed a man who would fight for her, who would break through her hesitation, who would show her that love—real love—was worth the risk.

And I failed to be that man.

I let her slip through my fingers.

And no matter how many years pass, no matter how many relationships follow, I will always wonder what life would have been like if I had held on just a little bit tighter.

9

One of a Kind Love Affair

When I broke up with Rachel, the hardest part wasn't the decision itself—it was letting go.

I had come so close to marriage that, in my mind, it felt like I had lost something valuable. I had invested time, energy, and emotion, and suddenly, it was gone.

Even though I knew ending things was the right decision, the illusion of loss haunted me.

I wasn't just mourning Rachel.

I was mourning the idea of Rachel.

And in those lonely days, every love song on the radio seemed to be speaking directly to me.

I was being pulled back to my younger years—those boarding school days when my friends and I would write love songs, dreaming about girls we had never met, imagining the kind of love that existed only in movies.

The breakup messed me up.

It shook the foundation of what I thought I wanted in a woman. It made me question everything I had valued in relationships.

And in many ways, reconnecting with Irene was a lifesaver.

She wasn't just another woman to date—she was a reminder.

A reminder that there were still women out there who could captivate me, challenge me, and restore my admiration for love itself.

The Wild Search for Love

But before Irene, before that reconnection, came the search.

In the months immediately after breaking up with Rachel, I moved to Houston, looking for a fresh start.

What I found was a disaster.

Dating in the church scene was horrifying.

Every date felt like an interview—not a conversation, not a moment to connect, but a structured assessment where I was being sized up as a prospective husband.

Gone were the innocent, carefree girls I had loved hanging out with in my youth.

These women came with a mission.

They weren't looking for romance or adventure or even a natural connection.

They were looking for security.

And maybe I couldn't blame them.

Most of them had probably been hurt before. Maybe they had experienced bad relationships that made them cautious, made them see marriage as a safe choice rather than an emotional one.

But for me?

It was suffocating.

I had always believed love should be organic, a gradual unfolding of mutual admiration and understanding.

Not a job application.

Not a checklist.

I realized that the church, for all its well-intentioned matchmaking, wasn't the right space for me to find what I was looking for.

I didn't want a woman searching for a husband.

I wanted a woman searching for me.

And that difference?

It made all the difference in the world.

The Reluctant Bachelor

The moment people realized I was single, everyone suddenly had someone they wanted to introduce me to.

It was as if my relationship status had become a public project—one that well-meaning friends, coworkers, and church members felt compelled to fix.

One day, a coworker approached me.

"Hey, you know, there's this girl I want to introduce you to."

I sighed inwardly. Oh my goodness, here we go again.

But instead of resisting, I agreed. Maybe—just maybe—this time would be different.

The girl was a student at LSU. We hit it off as friends, and I thought that was all it was—a friendship.

One evening, she called me, sounding stressed about some homework. She asked if I could help her out.

Of course, I agreed.

I went over, and we spent the evening going over her assignment. We drank coffee, worked through the problems, and by the end of it, she seemed relieved.

But then, something shifted.

I could feel it in the air.

She wanted to move the conversation to something else. Something personal.

I wasn't ready for that.

She asked if I liked her—if all the kindness I had shown her meant I was interested in something more.

I could feel my body tense.

I had been kind because… well, because I was kind.

Because she had asked for help, and I had been happy to offer it.

Not because I had some hidden romantic agenda.

I could feel the evening souring, and the more she pressed, the more agitated I became.

"I think of you as a friend," I told her. "That's why I helped you—not because I had any other intentions."

The conversation ended awkwardly.

I left feeling frustrated.

Driving home that night, a thought gnawed at me—was this what dating had become?

Had I become just another man being shuffled from one introduction to the next, each woman carrying her own expectations, her own agenda?

It wasn't fun anymore.

It wasn't natural.

And it became painfully clear:

I had lost interest.

I was desperate for a change.

Don't get me wrong—I appreciate the kindness of friends who try to set people up. There's nothing wrong with introductions.

But the problem with these setups is that they're built on assumptions.

People introduce you to someone because they think they know what you want. They assume compatibility based on shallow similarities—background, interests, or, in one particularly ridiculous case, geography.

One of my friends once introduced me to a woman simply because she also grew up somewhere in Africa.

Seriously?

As if location had anything to do with love.

That was the moment I knew—I needed to take back the initiative.

I was done with blind introductions, done with being passed around like some eligible bachelor waiting for the right woman to appear.

It was time to reconnect with people I already knew.

One of the old friends I reconnected with was Ciara.

We had met years ago at a barbecue in Houston when I first moved there, and we had stayed friends. She was easygoing, fun to be around, and didn't come with the weight of expectations.

So, when she invited me to visit her family in Mississippi, I figured—why not?

Since I was already in Baton Rouge, the drive wasn't too far. More importantly, there were no expectations.

No pressure.

No one sizing me up as a husband candidate.

Just two friends catching up.

But what happened next felt like déjà vu.

A Family Fight Again

During my visit, Ciara got into an argument with her sister right in front of their mother.

The scene took me straight back to Rachel's house on Thanksgiving, to the explosive argument between her and her sister, to the moment I naively stepped in and ended up taking the blame.

This time?

I stayed the hell out of it.

I sipped my drink, ignored the shouting, and kept my mouth shut.

Ciara noticed.

Later, she confronted me. She was upset that I hadn't defended her.

I could see where she was coming from. I was her guest. In her mind, I should have been on her side.

But I wasn't about to get pulled into family drama again.

I apologized, not because I thought I was wrong, but because I didn't want an argument.

To my surprise, she apologized too.

And just like that, the tension was gone.

That night, Ciara came to the guest room.

She was in her pajamas, looking relaxed, and without a word, she climbed onto the bed, sat cross-legged in the middle, and we just talked.

We talked all night.

It was effortless.

No pressure, no games, no pretense—just two people sharing stories, laughing, and enjoying each other's company.

And for the first time in a long time, I felt like myself again.

I felt like I was getting my mojo back.

Because these little things—late-night talks, laughing about the small stuff, pillow talk—these were the moments I missed most about relationships.

Not the grand gestures.

Not the romantic clichés.

But this.

Sitting in bed, talking about the comedy of the day, the highs and lows, the stupid little things that made life interesting.

This was what made love feel real.

And for the first time in a long time, I allowed myself to enjoy it.

A Weekend to Remember

I came back to Baton Rouge feeling lighter, more alive than I had in a long time.

And then, a few weekends later, Ciara came to visit.

It was the kind of weekend that reminded me why men love the company of a good woman—not for the grand gestures, but for the effortless joy of simply being together.

I had tickets for a college football game in New Orleans, so we drove down, the anticipation buzzing between us.

At the stadium, surrounded by roaring fans, I stole glances at her as she cheered on the home team with so much enthusiasm. She looked stunning.

She must have been the most beautiful woman at that game.

And I wasn't the only one who noticed.

I could feel the eyes of other men watching her, wishing they were in my shoes.

But she was with me.

And in that moment, I felt like the man of the moment.

As the game went on, the air grew chilly. I took off my jacket, draped it over her shoulders, and pulled her close.

She leaned into me slightly, a silent confirmation that she felt it too—that easy, simple magic of belonging to a moment.

I had missed this.

The warmth of having a woman by my side.

The simple pleasure of existing in the same space, without a care in the world.

An Evening for Just Us

After the game, we drove back to Baton Rouge.

I made dinner—something simple but comforting.

Afterward, we stretched out on the couch, music playing softly in the background.

Her head rested on my lap, her presence so natural, as if she had always belonged there.

We reminisced.

We talked about life, about dreams, about where we saw ourselves in the future.

She mentioned her love for London, how she had visited once and had completely fallen for the city.

"If I ever get engaged," she told me, "I want it to happen in London."

It was one of those small confessions people make in passing, but I remembered it.

The way she spoke about it, the way her eyes lit up—London meant something to her.

The night stretched on, peaceful and warm.

And as exhaustion caught up to me, my eyes grew heavy.

I bid her goodnight, pointed to the guest room, and made my way to bed.

A Moment of Misunderstanding

The next morning, when I woke up, I found her already awake, sitting quietly in the living room.

"I couldn't sleep," she said.

Surprised, I asked, "Oh. How come?"

She hesitated, then admitted, "I sat up wondering why you would go to bed alone and leave me out here by myself. I debated whether to come and lie down by you or not."

Her words caught me off guard.

For a brief moment, I considered explaining myself.

Ciara, I was tired, I almost said.

But before those words could leave my lips, I stopped myself.

I had learned from past relationships.

I had learned that some moments aren't about logic or excuses.

Some moments are about understanding—about respecting the unspoken between two people.

She thought I had missed an opportunity—that I had turned down a moment between us.

But the truth was, I had considered inviting her to bed with me.

Not out of expectation, not out of assumption, but because she was Ciara, and I respected her.

And because of that respect, I hesitated.

I didn't know how she would take it.

And the last thing I wanted was to insult her by being presumptuous.

When I finally did explain, she was momentarily taken aback.

But after a moment of reflection, she understood.

She hugged me tightly.

Then, with a big, warm kiss, she smiled, and without another word, she walked off to the guest room to change for the day.

It was enough.

She understood the kind of man I was.

And that mattered more than the moment itself.

She went back to Mississippi.

And we remained friends.

About six months after my return to New Jersey, life seemed to come full circle.

One evening, while walking through the city, I ran into Vanessa.

She was a girl from Tufts University—a girl I had once been madly in love with.

Seeing her again was like stepping into a familiar dream.

We decided to reconnect over dinner in the Village, and as we sat there, lost in conversation, I found myself feeling things I thought I had buried.

She was still so beautiful.

Still carried that effortless charm that had once captivated me.

And as we talked, she asked the inevitable question.

"Why are you still single?"

I sighed. There was no short answer.

So, I told her.

I told her about the past, about my relationships, about how none of them ever seemed to work out.

She listened carefully. Then, with a knowing smile, she leaned back and said:

"Boy, you have no idea what you want. Do you?"

Her words hit me like a punch to the gut.

Because she wasn't wrong.

Choosing Friendship Over Old Flames

She could see it—I missed her.

She could feel it—I was coming on to her without even realizing it.

But I had learned my lesson.

"There's just so much that has happened," I admitted. "All of it has gotten me confused, wary of getting into a relationship again. And as much as I like you—and would have liked to be in a relationship with you—I treasure your friendship. I'd much rather be friends."

For a moment, she studied me, her expression unreadable.

Then, she nodded.

She understood.

And just like that, we settled into the kind of friendship that doesn't carry the weight of what could have been.

A month later, she called me.

Her voice was light, happy.

"I have some good news."

"Oh yeah? Tell me."

"I got engaged."

I smiled.

And for the first time in a long time, I felt at peace with it.

When the Past Moves On

"Oh, wow—congratulations are in order then."

I said the words with a smile, but deep down, I felt a pang of something else.

It wasn't heartbreak. It wasn't regret.

But there was something about hearing Vanessa's news that stung.

She was one of the good ones.

And while I was genuinely happy for her, I couldn't ignore the small voice in my head that whispered, That could have been you.

Then, within the same month, Ciara called me.

She had also gotten engaged.

All of a sudden, it felt like all the women I had once loved were getting married.

Ciara's Dream Come True

I went to Ciara's wedding.

It was surreal, standing there, watching someone I had once shared so much with, walk down the aisle toward another man.

We found a moment to talk.

I congratulated her, asked her how she met her husband.

Her eyes lit up as she said, "You won't believe it—Martin is from London. He took me there to propose. It was so magical... my dream came true."

I forced a smile.

London.

She had always dreamed of getting engaged in London.

And now, some guy had come through for her.

Not me.

I felt sad.

And at the same time, happy for her.

Because that's what real love is, isn't it? Wanting the best for someone, even when that "best" doesn't include you.

I met her husband, Martin.

On the surface, he seemed like a nice enough guy.

But something about him didn't sit right with me.

He reminded me of the dog-pound guys I had known in the years when I had lost my way—men who had grown bitter toward women, men who saw relationships as transactional.

Martin came from a broken home, his parents had gone through a bitter divorce, and he carried himself with the air of a spoiled daddy's boy—a man who had never really faced hardship, never had to fight for anything.

As I watched him, something deep inside me whispered:

This marriage won't last.

But I said nothing.

Because sometimes, the things we see in people are not ours to say.

Some lessons, life teaches on its own.

Reflections on Love and Loss

Two years later, Ciara's marriage ended in divorce.

Her husband had an affair.

When I heard the news, I wasn't surprised—but I was sad.

Sad for Ciara, for the pain she had to endure, for the heartbreak that could have been avoided if only she had seen what I had seen.

As expected, Martin never made it out of the dog-pound.

He had been exactly who I feared he was—a man who wasn't ready for real commitment, a man who had never learned how to truly love.

When I thought about Vanessa and Ciara, I kept coming back to the same question.

How do women choose the men they marry?

Was it love?

A desire to settle down?

Or was it simply a matter of convenience?

I guess I would never really know.

But it made me reflect on my own journey.

I had been lucky—I had shared incredible moments with amazing women. I had loved deeply, learned so much, and even gotten engaged because I thought I was in love.

And yet, through all of it, I had never felt that absolute certainty—that undeniable knowing that this was the one.

I had always assumed that when the time was right, I would just know.

But now?

I wasn't so sure anymore.

Defining the One

So I sat down and thought about all the women I had been involved with.

What had I loved about them?

What had been missing?

And more importantly—what did I truly want in the woman I would spend forever with?

The answer didn't come in a checklist.

It didn't come in logic.

It came in words.

And so, I wrote them down:

> *Her voice I hear in time,*
> *Her face I behold in moments,*
> *She giggles gracefully*
> *as the song to her future begins.*
> *Pictures glory or none,*
> *Not grayed by the burdens of life,*
> *Color she possessed*
> *More than the pictures of old.*
> *More than wine, her water tastes,*
> *The face of humility*
> *And purity her water reflects.*
> *Her ways guided by wisdom,*
> *More than a friend she had been,*
> *A friend with a song,*
> *Never scared in the cold of winter.*
> *Dare I not see my reflection,*
> *A fine woman, which she is.*

This was the woman I was waiting for.

Not just someone to be with, but someone whose presence felt like home.

I had met incredible women.

But I had yet to meet her.

And so, I waited.

Because when she finally came into my life—I would just know.

I had memorized the poem long ago, carrying its words with me like a quiet prayer, whispering them to myself on long walks and first dates. It spoke of a woman whose presence wouldn't crash into my life with the force of a storm, but rather, settle into it like a soft, steady sunrise—graceful, unshakable, and quietly profound. She wouldn't captivate me with just beauty, wealth, or status, but with something deeper, something lasting. As the saying goes, "A woman's beautiful face attracts a flirter, a woman's beautiful heart attracts a lover, but a woman's beautiful character attracts a man." And I had reached the stage in my life where character mattered more than anything else.

After finishing business school, I joined Deutsche Bank in New York, trading long hours for the promise of success. It was around that time that a family friend introduced me to his cousin, a young woman he described as sweet, well-mannered, the kind of girl who could settle a restless heart. We talked on the phone for weeks, her voice light and warm, full of promise. Eventually, I invited her to visit, to step out from behind the safety of our calls and into real life.

The bank had leased a penthouse condo for me, a place that always seemed to impress my friends more than it did me. But when she finally arrived, stepping off the plane at LaGuardia, all of that faded into the background. She was breathtaking. The kind of beauty that made time slow down, that made you forget where you were.

Back at my place, she surprised me with a gift. It was unexpected, and for a brief moment, I let myself believe in the possibility—the thoughtfulness of it, the sweetness. But then I opened the box.

It wasn't a book or a keepsake, nothing sentimental or sincere. It was sex cream. And if that wasn't enough of a shock, she wasn't wearing any underwear either. Apparently, that was just her style.

The moment unraveled in an instant. The poetry, the quiet grace I had envisioned, it all vanished. I knew, without a doubt, that this wasn't the woman meant to bring peace into my life.

By morning, she was on a plane back home. And I was left standing at the airport, watching as the idea of her disappeared into the sky.

Not long after, I met Jules—a striking blonde with German ancestry, a woman whose elegance carried the effortless grace of an old Hollywood actress. She was slender, poised, the kind of woman who turned heads without even trying. From the moment we met, there was an ease between us, a natural rhythm that made friendship feel inevitable. And before long, friendship gave way to something more.

She reminded me of Vanessa in many ways—same height, same delicate frame—but there was something different about Jules, something more cinematic, as if she belonged on the silver screen rather than in a graduate seminar. She was loyal, open, and refreshingly direct. There was no pretense with her, no games. She knew what she wanted and had no hesitation in saying it. Maybe too soon.

One evening, with the city lights flickering in the distance, she took my hand and told me, without a hint of doubt, that she wanted to have my child. Her words hung between us, heavy with meaning, and I felt something shift inside me—uncertainty creeping in where certainty had once been.

It wasn't that I didn't care for her. I did. But Jules had lived a life before me, a complicated one. She had three children already, each with their own story. Her first husband had passed away, leaving her with memories of a love that had been stolen too soon. Her second marriage, however, had ended differently—fractured and bitter, tangled in the kind of heartbreak that left scars. The father of her youngest child was still out there, a lingering presence in her life, a shadow that couldn't be erased.

She had been honest with me from the start, laying out her past like an open book, giving me the chance to walk away before I ever walked in. But now, as the days turned into weeks and our relationship deepened, I found myself wrestling with an unease I couldn't ignore. The weight of her past, the complexity of what she wanted—it pressed against me in ways I wasn't sure I was ready for.

And so, as much as I had been drawn to Jules, as much as I admired her strength and honesty, I couldn't escape the quiet truth settling in my chest.

Something about it just didn't feel right.

Jules had told me about her ex-husband early on—how controlling he had been, how the marriage had unraveled under the weight of his temper. She spoke of the bruises he had left, the way he had tried to break her spirit, and though she was free of him in name, the reality was different. They shared a child, a permanent bond that neither of them could sever. And because of that, their battles hadn't ended with their divorce.

They still fought—loud, angry, heated arguments that flared up like sudden storms. I had listened as she dismissed them as nothing more than a lingering inconvenience, something she had learned to live with. But I wasn't convinced. A man like that didn't simply let go.

Then one night, my concerns became real.

We were at a restaurant, just the two of us, the hum of conversation around us a steady backdrop to our evening. And then, suddenly, he was there. Standing at our table, seething with barely contained rage, eyes burning with something wild and possessive. He had called her, she hadn't answered, and that alone had sent him over the edge.

The scene that followed was ugly—harsh words, sharp accusations, an atmosphere so thick with tension that the entire restaurant seemed to hold its breath. But what unsettled me most wasn't just his anger; it was the fact that he had found us. How had he known where we were? Was he watching her? Watching us?

A slow, cold fear settled into my bones.

Jules brushed it off later, saying he was just upset, that he wasn't a real threat. But I knew better. I had seen men like him before—the kind who let their fury simmer just beneath the surface, waiting for the moment it would boil over. She believed he would never go that far, that his threats were nothing more than empty echoes of a past she had already escaped.

But I wasn't willing to take that chance.

Infatuation is a powerful thing. It makes you believe in possibilities, in what could be, rather than what is. But even the most intoxicating love loses its sweetness when fear takes its place. A love that does not make you feel safe is not love—it is a dream teetering on the edge of a nightmare.

And so, despite the pull I still felt toward her, I knew I had to walk away. There was no changing the situation, no rewriting the story into something less complicated, less dangerous. Her past was always going to be a part of her present, and with it came a man who would never truly let go.

And I wasn't willing to gamble my peace—or my life—on the hope that he would.

The poem I had poured my heart into had become more than just words on a page—it was my compass, a quiet voice guiding me through the uncertainties of love and relationships. It reminded me of what truly mattered, whispering its truths when emotions threatened to cloud my judgment. Looking back at the relationships I had just recounted, I realized that, in the end, the poem had been right all along.

My parents had always told me that the choice of a partner was one of the most important decisions a person could make. The right person could anchor your life, build you up, make you better. The wrong one could unravel everything. Love wasn't just about passion or attraction—it was about choosing someone whose character could stand the test of time. A strong foundation wasn't just a romantic notion; it was the bedrock upon which a family was built. The culture in your home, the way you raised your children, the success or failure of the life you built together—it all came down to the kind of person you chose to dream with.

When Deutsche Bank transferred me to London, I found myself once again navigating the complexities of a new city, new faces, and new friendships. The rhythm of change had become familiar, but London held something different for me— memories of a woman who had once dreamed of this city.

Ciara.

She had always spoken about London with a kind of wistful longing, envisioning the perfect proposal in the heart of the city. And she had gotten it—just not with me. But her dream had turned into something else, something she hadn't expected. A nightmare.

I found myself wondering: If she had still been in my life, would we have taken that step? Would we have found ourselves in some candlelit corner of London, the moment unfolding just as she had imagined? The setting was perfect, yes—but had we ever been?

I suppose not.

Some dreams are meant to be, and others exist only to teach us something before they fade away.

I had begun to understand that memories weren't just remnants of the past—they were guiding lights, shaping my search for something real. Some women reminded me of the words in my poem, fragments of a dream I had long carried with me. Others made me want to rewrite it entirely, to add lines I had never considered before.

Then came that morning.

It was just past seven, the city still shaking off the quiet of dawn, and I was on my way to catch the train. That's when I saw her. She walked ahead of me, graceful, unhurried, as if the world moved at her pace, not the other way around. Something about her struck me—not in the obvious way that beauty does, but in a way that lingered. It was instinct, a pull, a feeling I couldn't quite place.

Curiosity got the better of me. I quickened my step, overtaking her just enough to steal a glance. And in that brief moment, something happened—I don't know if it was the way the morning light caught her face or the quiet confidence in her stride, but the image of her settled into me like a melody I couldn't forget.

The whole day, she stayed in my mind. I tried to shake it off, tried to focus on work, but the memory of her tugged at me relentlessly. By the afternoon, I had given in. I left work early, making my way back to the train station, hoping—praying—that I'd see her again.

And then, as if fate had been listening, she was there.

Standing on the platform, looking effortlessly radiant in the fading daylight. I walked up beside her, my pulse quickening, and said the simplest word I could think of.

"Hello."

She turned, and when she smiled, it was like the world had momentarily righted itself. There was something easy about her, something warm and inviting. We started talking, light and flirty, laughter slipping effortlessly between our words. In those few stolen moments, I could tell—she was alive in a way that people rarely were. She carried a spark, the kind that made you want to stand closer just to feel its warmth.

She was, in every way, the embodiment of my poem.

I wanted to know more. I wanted to ask her name, for her number, for anything that would allow me to see her again. But before I could, the train arrived, and in the hurried shuffle of bodies boarding, we were pulled apart.

And just like that, she was gone.

I searched for her every day after that, scanning the platform, watching for a glimpse of that familiar grace. The summer stretched on, and still, I never saw her again.

But she had left something behind—a memory so vivid, so inexplicably perfect, that she became more than just a passing stranger. In my mind, she became the living, breathing essence of my poem.

A fleeting moment. A whisper of what could have been.

The summer after my first year in London, I flew to Ghana for a two-week vacation with my father. It had been a while since I had spent any real time with him, and there was something grounding about being back home, away from the noise and distractions of my life abroad. One evening, as we sat outside under the quiet hum of the night, he turned to me with a suggestion I hadn't seen coming.

"Why don't you meet some women while you're here?" he asked casually, as though he were suggesting I try a new restaurant.

I laughed, shaking my head. "Dad, there's no way I'm agreeing to an arranged marriage."

He raised an eyebrow, unconvinced. "And why not?"

I could tell he was genuinely curious, so I humored him. "Because I have expectations, Dad. A lot of them. There are things I need to see, things I need to feel. And besides, I don't even live here. How am I supposed to know a woman's true character if we're miles apart? Long-distance relationships don't exactly do favors when it comes to figuring out who someone really is."

He nodded thoughtfully. Then, after a long pause, he asked the question I suppose any father would. "So tell me, what kind of woman are you looking for?"

I didn't answer right away. Instead, I reached into my pocket and pulled out a folded piece of paper—the poem. The one that had become my guide, the quiet blueprint of my heart's desire.

As I read it aloud, my father listened in silence, his expression unreadable. I told him about the women I had met, the experiences that had shaped these words, the countless ways in which I had searched for someone who would embody them.

When I finished, he exhaled slowly and gave me a long, knowing look.

"Well," he said at last, "I wish you the best in this search of yours. I just hope I live long enough to meet her. Although, at the rate you're going, I'll probably be in my grave before you find the woman of your dreams."

His words hung in the air between us, half-joking, half-serious. I chuckled, shaking my head, but something in his tone stayed with me.

Because as fate would have it, it wasn't long after that I met her.

10

You're All the World to Me

Before leaving Ghana, I spent my last day visiting a few old classmates from boarding school. We sat around, reminiscing about the past, swapping stories about where life had taken us. And then, inevitably, the conversation turned to marriage.

"Why aren't you married yet?" one of them asked, as if I had simply forgotten to tick it off my to-do list.

I smiled, shaking my head. "I haven't met the one."

He looked at me for a moment, considering my words. Then, with a knowing glint in his eyes, he said, "I think I have someone in mind."

I raised an eyebrow. "Oh yeah?"

"Yes, but…" he hesitated. "I need her father's permission before I can introduce you."

That caught my attention. It wasn't just the mystery of her, but the reverence with which he spoke. What kind of relationship did she have with her father that even a simple introduction required his blessing? It was rare to hear of something like that, and for reasons I couldn't quite explain, it piqued my interest.

A few hours later, my phone rang. My classmate had gotten the green light and sent me her number. "Call her," he said simply.

And so, I did.

She answered, her voice steady and calm, but there was a quiet weight behind it. When I introduced myself, she listened politely but wasted no time in telling me the truth.

"I appreciate the call," she said, "but I really don't have time to meet anyone right now. I recently lost my mother, and my father needs me. That's my priority."

Her words were gentle, spoken with grace, but there was no mistaking what she meant. She wasn't interested. Not now. Maybe not ever.

That was Grace.

Never had a woman been more fitting of her name.

I left Ghana the next day and returned to London, throwing myself back into work, life moving forward as it always did. But every now and then, I'd think of that brief conversation, of the woman who had so effortlessly embodied the kind of character I had always sought. A woman who knew what mattered, who carried love not just in words but in action.

Then, two months later, something unexpected happened.

My phone rang. And when I answered, it was her.

Grace.

And just like that, our story began.

Grace was the woman who made sense of everything. Every lesson, every heartache, every fleeting romance that had come before her—it all led to her, as if she had been waiting at the end of a long, winding road, the destination I hadn't even realized I was searching for.

Strangely enough, she carried echoes of the women from my past. She had Rachel's sweetness, Vanessa's fire, and Irene's undeniable allure. And yet, Grace was different. She didn't unsettle me or leave me questioning. She settled me. She didn't just fit the words of my poem—she became them.

Grace lived in the present, refusing to let past relationships or disappointments cast shadows over what we were building. Where others had been hesitant, where I had once struggled with uncertainty, Grace was unwavering. She made it clear, in both word and action, that she was fully committed to us. And with her, for the first time, I knew—without question, without doubt—that my feelings were truly reciprocated.

My parents adored her.

The first time they met her, she arrived dressed in traditional garb, a vision of quiet elegance and respect. My mother took one look at her and smiled, later whispering to me how beautifully and modestly she had presented herself. But it wasn't just her appearance—it was the way she carried herself. Grace had an instinctive understanding of people, of moments, of what mattered. She knew when to speak and when to listen, when to soften and when to stand firm. She moved through life with a quiet strength, a humility of heart that my mother would talk about for days.

For the first time, there was no hesitation, no second-guessing. My parents knew, as surely as I did, that Grace was the one.

She was my poem brought to life. And most importantly, she was ours.

I had been with women who were unafraid to voice their opinions—sometimes to the point of being brash. One had openly expressed her disappointment when I ended our date earlier than she had expected, making it clear that she had anticipated more from me. Another had outright asked if I was interested in marrying her before I had even had the chance to truly know her. And then there was the one who had fought with her family in front of me, turning what should have been a simple visit into a scene I wished I could erase.

Each of these encounters had left a mark, shaping the way I saw relationships, making me more aware of what I didn't want. And in doing so, they made me appreciate Grace even more.

Grace was modest, yet confident. She was refined, yet never rigid. She carried herself with the kind of effortless poise that made you take notice—not because she demanded attention, but because she simply was. She knew how to balance strength with softness, when to dress conservatively and when to make a statement, when to speak and when to let silence do the work. She was intelligent, breathtakingly beautiful, and a force of nature—calm as a summer breeze but capable of stirring the air with just her presence. She was something else entirely.

But what stood out most about Grace was her balance.

Unlike the women I had dated before, she was neither self-obsessed nor constantly seeking validation. She wasn't consumed by the material world, nor did she treat life as a stage where she always had to perform. With her, there was no pretense, no exhausting mind games. She didn't expect me to walk on eggshells when I complimented her, nor did she turn every conversation into a lesson on how I should better express my admiration. I still remembered one woman who had taken offense when I told her she looked good in her dress. She had scoffed and said, "I know I look stunning. I expected something more original from you."

With some of these women, I had felt like I was trapped in an unending lecture series—one where the syllabus was ever-changing, and I was always one lesson behind. The expectations were exhausting, leaving me questioning myself, feeling like I was never quite enough.

And yet, in the midst of it all, there were the ones who had taught me something valuable, who had refined my understanding of love and appreciation. In their own ways, they had led me here. To her.

To Grace.

She was the destination I hadn't realized I was searching for, the quiet reward after the storm. And for the first time, I didn't feel lost.

I felt home.

Grace was my safe haven. With her, I could breathe. I could be myself, wholly and without pretense, never feeling the need to put on an act or choose my words with caution. She never made me second-guess myself, never left me walking on a tightrope of unsaid expectations. With her, there was no fear of saying the wrong thing, no need to analyze and overanalyze every word spoken.

And her hugs—God, those hugs. They were warm, all-encompassing, the kind that made you feel like you belonged. And her smile? It was one of the brightest I had ever seen, the kind that could lift the heaviest of days and turn the ordinary into something extraordinary. It was pure joy being around her, a stark contrast to the times I had felt trapped in relationships that felt more like interrogations. Some of the women I had dated had scrutinized every statement, dissecting words until they no longer resembled their original meaning. Others found arguments in places where there were none, as if conflict were something to be nurtured rather than avoided.

That's not to say I hadn't had good times in my past relationships. There had been laughter, adventure, even moments of deep connection. But they were moments, fleeting and unpredictable, coming in waves that always seemed to recede too soon. With Grace, it was different. It was constant. Every day with her was filled with warmth, with joy, with an effortless happiness I had never quite known before.

And as I looked at her, at the woman who had effortlessly slipped into my life and into my heart, I realized something undeniable—my poem had finally taken flesh.

She was its embodiment, the living, breathing reward for all the searching, the waiting, the learning. Every word I had once written, every hope I had poured into those lines, had manifested in her.

My parents saw it too. They were convinced, without hesitation, that she was the one. And when my father finally gave me his seal of approval, I asked him how he knew with such certainty.

He smiled knowingly. "She listens more than she speaks," he said. "She has a kind word for everyone and is gracious to a fault. She carries a quiet charisma, and beyond being brilliant, she is emotionally wise. She has a depth that makes people feel at ease in her presence."

And he was right. Grace wasn't just remarkable—she was rare.

She became close to my parents in a way that felt natural, as if she had always belonged. To her, building a relationship with me meant building a relationship with my family, too. She understood something so many overlooked—that love isn't just about two people, but about the world they build together.

"If you ever meet a woman who only wants a relationship with you but has no interest in your family," my father once told me, "run."

With Grace, there was no running, no hesitation, no uncertainty. My mother adored her, my father respected her, and I—I was completely in love with her.

She had charmed us all. Not with grand gestures or calculated moves, but simply by being who she was.

Grace.

Six months after I introduced Grace to my parents, I made the call that would change my life forever.

I could have taken the simpler route—bought a ring, planned a private moment, and asked her to be my wife on my own terms. But that wasn't the kind of love she deserved. That wasn't the kind of respect her family deserved.

Grace had honored my family in ways I had never expected. She had embraced them as her own, showing them the kind of love and deference that spoke to the very core of who she was. And because of that, I knew that my love for her had to be reflected in my actions. If I was going to marry Grace, I was also marrying into her family. That's what my parents had always taught me—to love and honor not just the one we choose, but the family they come from, the people who shaped them into who they are.

And so, I asked my parents to go to her father and request her hand in marriage.

Her family accepted, and soon, a date was set.

Grace was the first woman I had ever loved without hesitation, without doubt, without second-guessing myself. She was the kind of certainty I had always longed for, the kind of peace I had once thought unattainable.

And so, on the day that would bind us forever, I stood at the altar, surrounded by my family, my friends, the people who had shaped my life, and waited for her.

Then, the music began—"The Sweetest Days" by Vanessa Williams.

The doors opened, and there she was.

Walking down the aisle, her arm linked with her father's, she looked up at me with a smile so radiant, so full of love, I felt its warmth settle deep in my soul. She was breathtaking. Ethereal. A vision of everything I had ever dreamed of and more.

Tears pooled in my eyes, my heart swelling with something indescribable. How had I gotten this lucky? How had I found this angel on earth?

And then, when the time came to place the ring on her finger, something inside me shifted. Without thinking, without hesitation, I dropped to my knees.

A hush fell over the room. The minister hesitated, momentarily perplexed. I could hear murmurs ripple through the guests, the quiet rustling of curiosity and confusion. It wasn't tradition, it wasn't planned—but in that moment, nothing mattered except her.

Because that was what my heart demanded.

A love like this didn't come around often, and Grace—my Grace—deserved every ounce of reverence I had in me.

And so, on my knees before her, in front of everyone who mattered, I offered her not just a ring, not just a promise, but the deepest, most profound truth of my heart.

It was a moment I would remember forever.

It wouldn't be wrong to say that without the many women who had come into my life before her, I might not have fully understood the importance of someone like Grace.

Each relationship had been a lesson, each experience shaping me in ways I hadn't recognized at the time. The fleeting romances, the moments of doubt, the uncertainty, the longing for something more—they had all been necessary. Because without them, I wouldn't have known just how rare and precious it was to find a woman who settled me, who loved me without conditions, without hesitation, without pretense.

Grace showed me the difference.

She made me realize the beauty of loving a woman and being loved in return—not with expectation or demand, but with a quiet certainty that left no room for doubt. With her, love wasn't something to be questioned or tested. It was simply there, steady and unwavering, like the most natural thing in the world.

And that—that—was the kind of love I had spent my life searching for.

This journey—my journey—began long before I even knew what love was. It started with a single moment, a spark, with a little girl in a hospital. A fleeting encounter that, unbeknownst to me, would set into motion a curiosity, a desire, a longing that would shape the course of my life.

That spark led me through a winding path of love and heartbreak, through lessons I never saw coming and experiences I hadn't always been ready for. I met women who challenged me, who tested me, who left me questioning myself. I learned what to do and what not to do, what to look for and what to overlook. Each woman left something behind—whether it was wisdom, pain, or the realization of what I truly wanted.

And in the end, that path led me to her.

To Grace.

As if fate itself had been orchestrating this journey, guiding me to the one woman who would make sense of it all. The woman who would be my home.

And as the gods would have it, Grace always looked breathtaking in red—bringing me full circle to that little girl in the hospital, the one who had unknowingly set my heart on its course all those years ago. I had finally graduated.

The lessons weren't always easy, and some of them had been painful. But I realized now that they had all been necessary. The women I had loved and lost, the moments of joy and heartbreak, had all polished and refined me into the man I was today—a man ready to commit, ready to love, ready to stand beside one woman for the rest of his life.

And that woman was Grace.

She was my final destination, my greatest lesson, my reward. And I? I was hers.

11

She Moves Me

From the moment I met Grace, something in me shifted. It wasn't an earth-shattering, love-at-first-sight kind of moment, but rather a quiet certainty that settled deep in my bones. My friends questioned how I could be so sure, why I had committed so quickly, but they didn't understand—how could they? Love isn't always about time; sometimes, it's about recognition. And my heart knew hers long before my mind could catch up.

With every conversation, every shared moment, I realized she was the missing piece I hadn't even known I was searching for. Loving her wasn't a choice; it was as natural as breathing. When I stood at the altar, watching her walk toward me, I felt the weight of something greater than myself. In that moment, I understood what it meant to be given a gift you could never deserve, to feel grace—not just as her name, but as a blessing woven into the fabric of my life.

As I spoke the words I do, I knew, without hesitation, that my life had changed forever. Because to love a woman like Grace— to be loved by her in return—was the greatest privilege of all.

After our wedding, I returned to London, and a week later, Grace followed, leaving behind the familiar comforts of Ghana to build a new life with me. Those early days in London were filled with laughter, love, and the kind of moments that make up the foundation of a marriage—the small, ordinary, yet unforgettable memories that shape a life together.

One of my favorites was our search for a place to call home. Since work kept me tied up, I had arranged for a realtor to help Grace with apartment hunting. Ever practical, she asked me what our monthly budget was, and in a moment of distraction—half-listening while buried in the chaos of my job—I absentmindedly gave her my entire monthly salary instead.

It wasn't until later, when she excitedly sent me listings of grand apartments in neighborhoods I'd never even considered, that I realized my mistake. You must really love me, she teased when I called her, laughing so hard I could hear the joy in her voice even through the phone.

And in that moment, as I listened to her, I knew that no matter where we lived—whether in a tiny flat or a grand estate—home had never been a place. It was Grace. It had always been her.

It was a monumental mistake. One moment, I was juggling deadlines at work, and the next, a realtor was calling to congratulate me on securing the perfect apartment—one Grace had already fallen in love with. Plans were already in motion, the paperwork nearly complete, and all that was left was my signature. She was thrilled, beaming as she told me how she had saved us so much money—half of what I had supposedly budgeted. That was the moment realization hit me like a freight train. I had given her my entire salary, not the budget I had in mind.

I gently pulled her aside, confessing my mistake in hushed tones. Her expression shifted from excitement to horror in an instant. But instead of making a fuss in front of the realtor—despite how much she adored the place—she simply nodded, turned back, and with all the grace that was so inherently her, told the realtor she had changed her mind.

That night, as we lay in bed, she turned to me, her voice soft but firm. You need to be clear in your communication, love. Otherwise, we might end up living in Buckingham Palace next time. There was no anger, no resentment—just wisdom, patience, and a quiet understanding that I had come to admire so deeply.

We settled on a smaller apartment in Central London, where we built the first chapter of our married life. For two years, we filled those walls with laughter, late-night conversations, and dreams about the future. And then, life shifted again.

A few years later, we made the decision to move to America—a fresh start, a new adventure. Grace wanted to further her education, and I was ready for a change, too. I had grown weary of the relentless grind of investment banking, so I resigned from my job at Deutsche Bank and accepted a position at a startup in Seattle. True to who she had always been, Grace supported me wholeheartedly, never once questioning my decision.

I flew ahead to Seattle, setting up a home for us, while Grace remained in London, needing to secure her American residency before she could join me. When I returned to London, we made our way to the U.S. Embassy, eager to take the next step.

The consulate approved her application, but there was a catch—processing would take months, meaning we would have to endure a painful separation until everything was finalized. As we walked out of the embassy, I could see the disappointment in her eyes. I reached for her hand, squeezing gently, searching for the right words to lift her spirits.

And then, as if fate had intervened, an elderly woman passed us in the hallway and stopped abruptly, her eyes lighting up as she took in Grace's outfit. Oh, my dear, that dress is simply stunning! Where did you find it?

Grace, ever the warm soul, smiled and struck up a conversation. The woman listened intently, nodding as we shared our reason for being there. And then, with a knowing smile, she reached for Grace's hand. I have a feeling everything will work out just as it should. Just you wait and see.

And in that moment, in the midst of an uncertain future, I saw Grace's smile return. Because somehow, in ways neither of us fully understood, life had a way of unfolding just as it was meant to.

The only hitch was time. Bureaucracy had its own pace, and we were told it would take a few months before Grace could join me. I had to leave immediately, which meant weeks—possibly months—of separation. The thought of it weighed on both of us, but we had no choice.

The woman listened, nodding with understanding, and then, as if it were the simplest thing in the world, she turned to Grace and said, Why don't you stop by for a chat in a couple of weeks?

And so Grace did.

And guess what? Her application had been approved.

That woman—the one who had stopped to compliment her dress—was no ordinary stranger. She was a senior official at the embassy, and with a quiet kindness that changed everything, she had fast-tracked the process.

A guardian angel? Perhaps. Or maybe it was simply Grace—her warmth, her effortless way of drawing people in, of making them want to help her, be near her. Whatever it was, all I knew was this: my wife was coming home to me.

When Grace landed at Seattle SeaTac Airport, I was already counting the seconds until I could hold her again. And as if fate was determined to make up for lost time, her residency was approved right there at the airport, in less than two hours.

No more waiting. No more distance.

We were finally together in America, stepping into a new chapter of our lives. Our apartment in Seattle was nearly empty, except for one thing—a mattress on the floor. I hadn't set up much while waiting for her, wanting us to build our home together.

And so we did.

We laughed as we picked out furniture, turned bare walls into something that felt like us, and spent our first nights in that nearly empty apartment wrapped in the warmth of simply being together. It felt like a honeymoon all over again—only this time, it wasn't just a moment. It was the beginning of forever.

Life in Seattle settled into a rhythm, one that felt both new and familiar at the same time. Grace signed up for classes at the local community college, eager to build something of her own, while I poured every ounce of energy into the startup, working insane hours that left me drained.

But no matter how exhausted I was at the end of the day, I always came home to Grace. To warmth. To laughter. To a home she had carefully built, not just with furniture and décor, but with love, with patience, with the kind of tenderness that made all the stress and chaos of the outside world melt away the moment I walked through the door. She was my safe place. My refuge. My home.

And then, one day, our home expanded.

The news that we were becoming parents shifted everything between us in the most beautiful way. Suddenly, our late-night talks were filled with baby names, nursery ideas, and dreams about the little life we were about to bring into the world. The pregnancy became the first true test of reality in our marriage, and let's just say—it came with its fair share of surprises.

Grace's cravings sent me on wild goose chases all over Seattle, hunting down the most absurd food combinations at the oddest hours. One night, she had to have mango sorbet and jalapeño chips. Another, it was pancakes from a specific diner—one that was inconveniently closed. But I never minded, not really. My love for her made every errand, every exhaustion-induced drive across the city, worth it.

And then, finally, the big day arrived. Or at least, we thought it had.

Our son, it seemed, wasn't in a hurry to leave the comfort of his mother's womb. We had nearly ten false alarms—each one sending us rushing to the hospital, only to be sent back home again. By the time Grace was actually in labor, I almost missed it entirely.

I had rushed home to grab a few things she had forgotten, thinking I had plenty of time. But just as I stepped through our front door, my phone rang.

It was Grace.

Her voice was breathless, urgent. You need to come back. Now.

And in that moment, nothing else mattered. Not the startup, not the exhaustion, not even the months of waiting. The only thing that mattered was getting back to her. Because the next time I saw her, our lives would change forever.

"Where are you? I think he's finally coming!"

Grace's voice rang through the phone, laced with panic, urgency, and something else—something that made my heart slam against my ribs. This was it.

I don't know how I made it back to the hospital without getting pulled over. In hindsight, it was a miracle I didn't crash, considering how fast I was driving, how hard my hands gripped the steering wheel, white-knuckled with adrenaline and fear and anticipation all rolled into one.

I burst through the hospital doors just in time. Just in time to see her, to take her hand, to whisper words of encouragement even as I was barely holding myself together. And then—finally—he was here.

Our son.

The second I held him, the world around me blurred. The exhaustion, the stress, the countless false alarms—it all faded into something distant, something insignificant. Because in my arms was the most perfect, most incredible little human I had ever laid eyes on.

He was ours.

Grace, through the sheer force of love and strength and everything that made her extraordinary, had given me this impossible, precious gift. And as I looked at his tiny hands, his impossibly small feet, I knew one thing for certain—I would spend the rest of my life trying to be worthy of this moment, of them.

I turned to Grace, my heart so full it ached, and wrapped her in my arms. I kissed her, whispered a thousand thank yous against her skin, though none of them would ever be enough. Because how do you thank someone for giving you everything?

Back home, the reality of it all hit me in the quietest, most unexpected way.

Tiny clothes and baby socks hung off the bathroom racks, the scent of baby powder lingering in the air. I stared at them, at this small, ordinary snapshot of our new life, and something inside me broke wide open.

I sank onto the bathroom floor and wept.

Not from exhaustion, not from fear, but from overwhelming gratitude. Because in that moment, in the soft hum of our home, I realized just how profoundly, how undeservingly blessed I was.

That first night, as his cries echoed through our home, I felt it all over again. The weight of fatherhood. The enormity of love.

I never imagined anyone could bring me this much joy. But that was Grace. Ever extraordinary, ever radiant. She was my anchor, my clarity, my calm in the storm. And now, she had given me the greatest gift of all—our son. A piece of her. A piece of us.

And for the rest of my life, I would never stop thanking her for it.

My love for Grace had always been deep, unwavering—but in the moments that tested us, that love transformed into something even stronger, something unshakable. And nothing tested us more than the night we thought we were losing our son.

He had always been a fussy baby, crying more than our firstborn ever had. But that night—that night—was different. We heard a crack. A sickening, unmistakable sound that sent us into full-blown panic. He was only six months old.

We rushed him to Seattle Children's Hospital at 8:00 p.m., my heart pounding so hard I could barely breathe. Hours passed in a blur of sterile rooms and hushed conversations until a group of doctors finally approached us. Their faces were heavy with something I didn't want to name.

"All signs point to bone cancer," one of them said.

The words knocked the air from my lungs. Bone cancer. Our baby.

I was already breaking apart, already searching for a way to make it better, to fix it, to trade places with him if I could. So when they asked for my consent to extract bone marrow for further testing, I was ready to sign—anything, everything—if it meant saving my son.

But then, Grace.

She reached out, her hands warm against mine, grounding me. Her voice was calm, steady—so sure that it silenced the chaos inside me.

"We would like a second opinion, please. Our son does not have bone cancer. You have to run your tests again."

The doctors exchanged looks, insisting they had already run and rerun the tests. The results hadn't changed. But Grace wasn't swayed. She didn't raise her voice, didn't falter. She simply refused.

She asked to see another doctor.

They told us the Head of Oncology was away on vacation. If we wanted his opinion, we would have to wait.

So we waited.

Days turned into weeks, and through it all, Grace remained unshaken. While I was unraveling, she held fast to her faith. She prayed. She believed. She was an oasis of calm in the storm threatening to drown us.

Two weeks later, the call finally came. The Head of Oncology had returned.

We met him expecting another whirlwind of medical jargon and statistics, but instead, we found an older man with kind eyes and a patience that felt reassuring. He listened as we told him everything—what had happened, what the other doctors had said. He nodded, asked a few careful questions, then excused himself to review the test results.

When he returned, his gaze fell on Grace first.

"You were right, Ma'am," he said, his voice filled with something close to admiration. "There is nothing wrong with your son."

Relief crashed over me so forcefully I could barely stand.

I turned to Grace, overwhelmed. She had been right. She had known. Not through science, not through logic, but through the quiet, unwavering certainty of a mother's love.

I pulled her close, burying my face against her shoulder, breathing her in.

She had saved our son.

And in that moment, I knew—whatever storms life threw our way, I would never stop trusting in her, never stop being in awe of her. Because Grace wasn't just my wife. She was my anchor, my guiding light. And she always would be.

Six doctors. Six trained, experienced professionals—all of them had been wrong. And Grace, my Grace, had been right.

They had misdiagnosed our son, sent us spiraling into a nightmare that never should have existed. But because of her, because of her unwavering belief, her quiet strength, and the way she never let fear dictate her choices, we had found our way back to the truth.

I looked at her that day, sitting beside me in that hospital room, and all I could feel was gratitude so deep it made my chest ache.

What had I ever done to deserve her?

Her wisdom, her kindness, her instinct—they weren't just qualities I admired; they were the very foundation of our life together. I had leaned on them more times than I could count, had been saved by them in ways big and small.

And today, seventeen years later, our son—the same boy we once feared might be slipping away from us—is strong, healthy, and full of life. A reminder every single day of how close we came to believing something that wasn't true. A reminder of Grace's unwavering love.

I've spent years learning that listening to her, turning to her, is the single greatest decision I could ever make—whether in moments of ease or in the depths of uncertainty. She has been my greatest blessing, my truest north.

And as I look at her now, after all these years, I know one thing beyond a shadow of a doubt.

It feels so good to love this woman.

12

Home Ain't My Heart

It started with Grace. It always started with her.

Loving her was easy—so easy, in fact, that I often wondered if love had been waiting for me in her all along. She taught me things I hadn't known before, things my father had only hinted at in his quiet, steady way. That companionship was more than passion. That devotion was more than just a promise. That love, real love, wasn't about grand gestures or whispered confessions under moonlit skies, but about showing up—day after day, even when it was hard.

I'd known other women before her, but none like Grace. She was magic wrapped in kindness, the kind of person who made you want to be better, not because she asked, but because loving her made you believe you could be. My father had always told me that intimacy should come with commitment, that a man should never share his soul with someone he couldn't hold in the light of day. My best friend, Arthur, had told me something similar—that love meant accountability, that if you truly cared for someone, you answered to them. Both men had shaped the way I loved Grace. Both had given me the wisdom I carried into our marriage.

And then, just like that, I lost them.

Seattle had begun to wear on us. The rhythm of work, of raising children, of bills and responsibilities, had dulled the shine of the life we'd built. I was always gone. Grace was always holding everything together. And then the worst of it—my father, my anchor, suffered a stroke and was gone before I had the chance to say goodbye. I grieved, but grief has a way of reshaping everything you believe in, and for me, it left cracks in the foundation.

Arthur, my friend, my trusted confidant in all things love and marriage, got divorced. The man I had leaned on for advice, the man who had always known the right thing to say, was suddenly alone. It shook me in ways I didn't understand. If Arthur, the man who had always believed in love, could lose it—then what chance did any of us have?

Grace saw it happening—the way I started drifting, the way I let despair creep into the spaces where love used to live. She tried. God, she tried. But I was slipping, and even though I could see it breaking her, I didn't know how to stop it.

We left Seattle, hoping that a new place would mean a new beginning. Oregon, with its open skies and fresh air, should have been enough. But it wasn't. So we tried again—Connecticut this time, hoping that somewhere along the way, we'd find our way back to each other.

It was there that I found another father figure—Grace's father. He stepped in when I needed someone to steady me. He was a man of quiet wisdom, a lighthouse in the storm of my uncertainty. I wrote to him often, seeking guidance, and he always had an answer. But life, as I'd come to understand, had a cruel way of taking the things I loved most.

When he fell ill in Ghana, I went to him, leaving Grace behind because she was carrying our last child and couldn't travel. I held his hand, felt the frailty in his grip, and he looked at me the way my own father once had.

"Take care of Grace," he said softly. "And she will always take care of you."

I didn't know it then, but those were the last words he'd ever speak to me.

When he was gone, I felt that loss as deeply as all the others before it. But what I hadn't seen—what I'd been too consumed by my own grief to notice—was that Grace was breaking too. She had lost her father, the man who had been her guiding light, and I hadn't been there to hold her through it. We grieved alone, instead of together. And that was when the real fractures started.

Small fights. Distance. A quiet unraveling.

I thought moving again would fix it. London, this time. Another fresh start, another chance to run away from the things we didn't want to face. The plan was for me to go first, to settle in, and then send for her and the boys. It was a mistake—one I will regret for the rest of my life.

We should have stayed. We should have fought for what we had instead of hoping that distance would heal the wounds we refused to look at. Because miles don't mend broken things; they only stretch the cracks wider.

I lost myself in work. Grace lost herself in the chaos of raising three boys alone, grieving her father, missing me in ways I hadn't even begun to understand. And though we survived it— though we held on by the thinnest of threads—I wonder, even now, if love, no matter how deep, can ever truly withstand the weight of so much loss.

But this I know—home isn't a place. It never was.

Home is Grace.

And I only pray I'm not too late to find my way back to her.

Looking back, I suppose I always knew Grace would be the one to hold everything together. She was the steady rhythm beneath the chaos, the quiet strength I leaned on without even realizing it. While I was in London, living alone in a hotel room with only the hum of the city outside my window to keep me company, she was everything to our children—both mother and father, their protector and provider. She made sure they were safe, that they learned, that they had a home filled with love, even in my absence. And somehow, in the midst of it all, she still found the time to chase a dream of her own.

She went to culinary school, pouring her heart into flour and sugar, kneading her emotions into dough, turning grief and longing into something tangible—something sweet. And, God, let me tell you, her pastries were something else. The kind that melted in your mouth, that tasted like home.

I should have known then that Grace was the kind of woman my father had always told me to find—the kind who didn't flinch when life got hard, who worked with her hands, who took charge when the weight of the world threatened to crush her. I had seen it before, in the way she loved me, in the way she stood beside me through every storm. But sometimes, love blinds you to the very things you should have seen all along.

And then I got sick.

It started with a sharp pain in my stomach—nothing I thought much of at first. But when the pain didn't go away, I went to see a doctor. Tests were run. Conversations were had. And then, the words I never expected to hear.

Cancer.

Even now, I can still remember the way the world seemed to tilt beneath me, how the air in that sterile white office felt too thin, how the memory of another hospital room—another life-changing moment—came rushing back to me. The day we sat there, hand in hand, when the doctors gave us the news about our son. That same fear clawed at me now, only this time, it was my life hanging in the balance.

I needed Grace.

I needed the quiet way she steadied me, the way she could take even the worst news and turn it into something bearable. So I did the only thing that made sense. I got on the next flight back to Connecticut. Back to my wife. Back to the only place that had ever truly felt safe.

When I told her, she didn't cry. She didn't panic. She took my hands in hers, looked me in the eyes, and said, "We're going to get through this. But first, we're getting a second opinion."

That was Grace. Always practical. Always ready to fight, even when I didn't have the strength to.

The urologist confirmed what the first doctor suspected—prostate cancer. And suddenly, I was facing something I had no idea how to prepare for. The fear, the uncertainty, the slow unraveling of everything I had built inside my head. But Grace was there, like she had always been. The one constant in my ever-changing world.

It was a battle, one of the hardest I'd ever fought. But I wasn't fighting alone.

Because I had Grace.

That day, after my appointment with the doctor, the weight of it all became too much. The fear, the uncertainty, the thought of everything I could lose—it came crashing down on me in a way I couldn't hold back. I broke. I wept like a man who had run out of places to run, like someone who had finally realized just how fragile life truly was.

And Grace—my Grace—held me.

She didn't tell me to be strong. She didn't tell me everything would be fine. She simply wrapped her arms around me, held me close, and whispered, "I'm here. We will get through this. Together."

It was in that moment that I understood something I should have known all along. I was home.

Not in the house we lived in, not in the cities we had traveled to, not in the new beginnings we had chased across the world. Home wasn't a place. Home had never been a place.

Home was this woman. This strong, beautiful, gracious woman who had stood beside me through every storm, who had held on to me even when I had nearly let go. Home was in the quiet way she loved me, in the unwavering way she believed in me, in the way she carried me when I no longer had the strength to stand on my own.

After everything—the years of searching, the lessons learned from love lost and found, the winding road that had led me to her—I knew, without a doubt, that she was the one I had been searching for all along.

Grace wasn't just my wife. She wasn't just the mother of my children.

She was my heart. My safe place. My beginning and my end.

And loving her?

Loving her was the easiest thing I had ever done.

She taught me so much in our years together—about honesty, responsibility, resilience, love. But there was one thing, one truth so simple yet so profound, that she had given me above all else.

It is so good to love a woman.

And God, how good it is to love her.

I am completing this book just one week after saying goodbye to my dear mother. She lived eighty-eight full, beautiful years, and though I know she is at peace, the loss still lingers, settling deep in the quiet spaces of my heart.

As I sit here, looking back at my life with her—the warmth of her laughter, the lessons she imparted, the unwavering love she gave me—I see now that Grace has been nothing but a continuation of the blessings that Providence has so graciously placed in my path.

My mother was the first woman I ever loved, the one who taught me what love should feel like. She showed me kindness, strength, and sacrifice in the simplest of ways—through a touch, a look, a presence that was always steady, always there. And then, years later, I found Grace. Or perhaps, Grace found me.

I have been given the rarest of gifts—the chance to love and be loved by two extraordinary women. A mother who shaped me, and a wife who became my home.

And if there is one thing I know to be true, one thing I have learned through it all, it is this:

It is so good to love a woman.

About the Author

Ohene Aku was born in the coastal town of Elmina, on the west coast of Africa, to an English schoolteacher mother and a civil servant father who dedicated his life to Ghana's timber industry. His parents built a love that lasted over fifty years—a love that stood firm through time, through trials, through the quiet, ordinary moments that make a lifetime. It was only with the passing of his father that their long chapter together came to an end.

From that small town by the sea, Ohene Aku's journey took him across the world, to the halls of the Massachusetts Institute of Technology, where he spent his academic years shaping his mind, forging the foundation for a future he could scarcely have imagined as a boy. But it wasn't just intellect or ambition that carried him forward—it was something more.

After graduating, as a single man navigating the corridors of corporate America and the vast cities of the world, he found himself drawn into the high-stakes world of Wall Street. Success came, challenges followed, and the years passed in a whirlwind of numbers, boardrooms, and flights across continents.

But through it all, one truth remained—his life had been shaped, nurtured, and enriched by the women who crossed his path.

The story he has set out to tell in this book is not just a recounting of moments, but a tribute—an ode to the quiet magic that too many men overlook. In chasing success, in seeking power, they often miss the very thing that gives life its deepest meaning.

Ohene Aku paid attention.

He watched. He listened. He learned.

And in the end, he did something far greater than merely admire women—he fell in love with womanhood itself.

www.ingramcontent.com/pod-product-compliance
Lightning Source LLC
Chambersburg PA
CBHW060319030426
42336CB00011B/1114